MY EXPERIENCES
AS AN EXECUTIONER

By

JAMES BERRY

First published in 1892

Read & Co.

Copyright © 2020 Read & Co. History

This edition is published by Read & Co. History,
an imprint of Read & Co.

This book is copyright and may not be reproduced or copied in any
way without the express permission of the publisher in writing.

British Library Cataloguing-in-Publication Data
A catalogue record for this book is available
from the British Library.

Read & Co. is part of Read Books Ltd.
For more information visit
www.readandcobooks.co.uk

CONTENTS

4

ON ANNE GREEN, HER EXECUTION

By John Mainard

Sure Death abhorres the colour, all have seene
that Death is blacke, and therefore loves no Greene:
A happy colour, in what Prædicament
Will the Logicians put this Accident?
Shee had her Neck-verse; 'tis a currant signe
Shee could not read, her verse was but a Line.
Againe, upon this deed to set a crowne;
Sh'ad been cut up, if not so soon cut downe.
Read this thou youthfull, Read, and be afraid.
Shee's a maid twice, and yet is not dis-maid.
O Paradoxe! if truth in thee can lye
No wonder if the maid could live and dye.

James Berry

INTRODUCTION

THE intention of both the author and the editor of this little book has been to set forth, as plainly and as simply as possible, certain facts and opinions with regard to what is undoubtedly a most important subject—the carrying out of the ultimate sentence of the law. While facts have not been in any way shirked or misrepresented, much that is horrible in detail has been suppressed; so that people who may be tempted to take up the book in search of ghastly descriptive writing, are warned at the outset that they will be disappointed.

It is believed that a publication of Mr. Berry's experiences will correct many errors and misconceptions as to the way in which capital sentences are carried out in England; and that it will lead to a consideration of the whole subject, from a practical, rather than from a sentimental, point of view.

The management, and, if possible, the regeneration of the criminal classes, is one of the most serious tasks that civilisation has to face; and those who undertake such a task require all the light that can possibly be thrown upon the subject. The public executioner has many and special opportunities of studying the criminal classes, and of knowing their attitude and feelings with regard to that capital punishment which civilisation regards as its strongest weapon in the war against crime. When, as in the case of Mr. Berry, several years' experience in various police forces can be added to his experience as an executioner, the man who has had these exceptional opportunities of studying criminals and crime, must necessarily have gathered much information and formed opinions that are worthy of attention.

Therefore, this book has a higher aim than the mere recording of the circumstances and incidents of the most painful business in which a man can engage. The recording is necessary, for without the facts before them, readers could not form their own opinions; but it is hoped that the facts will be read with more than mere curiosity, that the readers will be led to take a personal interest in the weak and erring brethren who form the criminal classes, the canker-worm of our social system.

An explanation of how this book was written may not be out of place. The statements are *entirely* those of the author, though in many cases the words are those of the editor, whose task consisted of re-arranging and very greatly condensing the mass of matter placed in his hands by Mr. Berry. The narrative and descriptive portion of the work is taken from a series of note-books and a news-cuttings book kept by Mr. Berry; who includes the most minute particulars in his diaries. One chapter—"My First Execution"—is word for word as written in the diary, with the exception that a few whole pages of descriptive detail are omitted, and indicated by points (thus . . .) The chapter "On Capital Punishment," and portions of other chapters, were not written out at length by Mr. Berry, but were supplied in the form of full notes, and the principal portions dictated. In every case, however, the opinions are those of the author, with whom the editor is by no means in entire personal agreement.

MY EXPERIENCES AS AN EXECUTIONER

CHAPTER I

THE EXECUTIONER AT HOME
BY H. SNOWDEN WARD

JAMES Berry, though regarded by some people as a monster, and by others as a curiosity, is very much like any other working-man when one comes to know him. He is neither a paragon of perfection, nor an embodiment of all vice—though different classes of people have at times placed him under both these descriptions. His character is a curious study—a mixture of very strong and very weak traits, such as is seldom found in one person. And although one of his weak points is his Yorkshire open-hearted frankness, which he tries to control as much as possible, the man who has only been with him a few days has not by any means got to the depths of his character. His wife has said to me more than once:—"I have lived with him for nineteen years, but I don't thoroughly know him yet," and one can quite understand it, as his character is so many-sided and in some respects contradictory. This partly accounts for the varying and contradictory views of his personality which have been published in different papers.

His strongest point is his tender-heartedness. Perhaps this

may be doubted, but I state the fact from ample knowledge. Mr. Berry's occupation was not by any means taken up from a love of the ghastly, or any pleasure in the work. Even in his business as executioner his soft-heartedness has shown itself, for though it has never caused him to flinch on the scaffold, it has led him to study most carefully the science of his subject, and to take great pains to make death painless.

Of this trait I have had many proofs. For instance, I know that on some occasions when he has been due to start for a place of execution, his repugnance to the task has been so great that his wife and her mother have been obliged to use the greatest possible force of persuasion to prevent him shirking his duty. Another instance of this characteristic appeared when I was overhauling his manuscript and cuttings for the purpose of this book. I came across a copy of a poem "For one under Sentence of Death," and made some enquiry about it. I found that the lines were some which Mr. Berry had copied from a Dorchester newspaper, and that for a long time it had been his habit to make a copy of them, to send to the chaplain in every case where a prisoner was sentenced to death, with a request that they should be read to the prisoner. This was continued until the governor of one of the gaols resented the sending of such a poem to the chaplain, and intimated that in all cases the chaplain was best able to judge of what was necessary for the condemned man, and did not need any outside interference. After this Mr. Berry sent no more poems, but he kept one or two copies by him, and I think that it may interest the reader.

LINES FOR ONE
UNDER SENTENCE OF DEATH

My brother,—Sit and think,
  While yet some hours on earth are left to thee;
Kneel to thy God, who does not from thee shrink,
  And lay thy sins on Christ, who died for thee.

He rests His wounded hand
  With loving kindness, on thy sin-stained brow,
And says—"Here at thy side I ready stand,
  To make thy scarlet sins as white as snow.

"I did not shed My blood
  For sinless angels, good and pure and true;
For hopeless sinners flowed that crimson flood,
  My heart's blood ran for you, my son, for you.

"Though thou hast grieved me sore,
  My arms of mercy still are open wide,
I still hold open Heaven's shining door,
  Come then—take refuge in My wounded side.

"Men shun thee—but not I,
  Come close to me—I love my erring sheep.
My blood can cleanse thy sins of blackest dye,
  I understand, if thou canst only weep."

Words fail thee—never mind,
  Thy Saviour can read e'en a sigh, or tear;
I came, sin-stricken heart, to heal and bind,
  And died to save thee—to My heart thou'rt dear.

11

Come now—the time is short,
 Longing to pardon and to bless, I wait;
 Look up to Me, My sheep so dearly bought,
 And say, "forgive me, e'er it is too late."

E. B. C.

The soft-heartedness of Mr. Berry's nature would quite unfit him for his post if it were not that he possesses a strong resolution, and can control his feelings when he finds duty warring against inclination.

In personal appearance he is a kindly-looking man, thickset and muscular, with a florid complexion and sandy hair. He stands 5ft. 8½in. high, weighs 13 stones, and does not look the sort of man to willingly injure anyone. The appearance of his right cheek is somewhat marred by a long, deep scar, extending downwards from the corner of the eye, which has given rise to one or two sensational stories from the pens of imaginative newspaper men. The scar was caused by the kick of a horse which he attempted to ride when he was a boy about ten years old. The horse was young, unbroken and vicious, and its kick narrowly missed being fatal. Across his forehead is another great scar, the result of a terrible blow received when arresting a desperate character in a Bradford public-house. The man was one of a gang of six, and his comrades helped him to violently resist arrest, but Berry stuck to his captive until he was safely locked in the Bradford Town Hall, and the six men all had to "do time" for the assault.

Mr. Berry was born on February 8th, 1852, at Heckmondwike, in Yorkshire. His father was a wool-stapler, holding a good position in the district. Young Berry's education was obtained at the Wrea Green School, near Lytham, where he gained several prizes for his writing and drawing. His writing ability was useful to him later in life, when he was employed by a lithographer, to write "copper-plate" transfers. In 1874 he was married, and has had six children. Of these, two boys and a girl died while young, and two boys and a girl are living.

The "executioner's office," as Mr. Berry likes to call it on his official communications, is a house just off City Road, Bradford. It is one of six owned by Mr. Berry. When he first took the position of executioner some of his neighbours were so prejudiced against the work, that they refused to live "next door to a hangman," and as landlords naturally object to losing two or three tenants for the sake of keeping one, Mr. Berry was obliged to move once or twice, and came to the conclusion that he had better be his own landlord. The prejudice which then existed has been lived down, and there is now no difficulty in letting neighbouring houses to respectable tenants.

The house in Bilton Place is furnished just the same as hundred of other houses in the district that are occupied by better-class artisans, and there is nothing at all gloomy or gruesome about the place. In fact, there is no indication of the business of the occupant. There are, in the front room, two frames of small photographs, which are really portraits of some of the murderers who have been executed by Mr. Berry, but the frames bear no inscription. In a glass-fronted sideboard, too, there are a few handsome electro goblets, cruet stands and similar articles that have been given to Mr. Berry by some of his admirers, but no one would connect them with his business. In drawers and cupboards about the place there are (or were, for they have now gone to Madame Tussaud's) a large number of relics and mementos of executions and other incidents. Amongst them is the great knife, once used by the executioner of Canton for the beheading of nine pirates. This was obtained in exchange for a rope with which several persons had been hanged. These relics were all stowed well away, and were not by any means "on show," though the executioner did not object to producing them if a personal friend wished to see them.

In conversation Mr. Berry is fluent, apt in anecdote and illustration, and full of a subtle Yorkshire humour which he cannot entirely shake off even when talking on serious subjects. He has a very good memory for facts, and is very observant, so that he is always ready with a personal experience or observation on almost any topic. His tastes are simple. His favourite occupations are fishing and otter hunting, of both of which sports he is passionately fond. Frequently when going to an execution in a country town he takes his rod and basket, and gets a half-day's fishing before or after the execution. He seems to like the sport on account of its quiet and contemplative nature, and says that he enjoys the fishing even if he never gets a nibble.

At home Mr. Berry devotes himself largely to mechanical pursuits. At the present time he is working a patent which he bought recently, and has the topmost room of his house fitted as a mechanic's workshop, with lathe, bench, etc. In spare time he devotes a good deal of attention to his pigeons and rabbits, for he is an ardent fancier, and keeps a large number of live pets.

CHAPTER II

HOW I BECAME AN EXECUTIONER

IT has been said by some of those goody-goody moralists who are always anxious to point out sad examples of the depravity of man, and who are not very particular about the genuineness of the "facts" with which they support their theories, that I was fond, even as a boy, of revelling in the revolting details of crime, and that I was a reader of all the police literature that I could obtain. Such statements are absolutely false. As a boy I was not a great reader on any subject, and the proceedings of the courts and the careers of criminals were in no wise interesting to me until I became a member of the Bradford Borough Police Force, in 1874.

When a policeman I strove to do my duty as well as any man could, and often wished that I could make some better provision for my wife and family, but I never so much as dreamed of becoming an executioner, or took any interest in the subject of hanging.

One day, when I called at a friend's house that was on my beat, it happened that Mr. Marwood was staying there, and I was introduced to him, and a few days later I again met him and spent an evening in his company. He was a quiet, unassuming man, kindly and almost benevolent in his manner, who was in no way ashamed of his calling, though very reticent about speaking of it, excepting to those whom he knew well. He keenly felt the odium with which his office was regarded by the public, and aimed, by performing his duties in a satisfactory manner, and by conducting his private life respectably, at removing the stigma which he felt was undeserved. At times the attitude of the public towards him was very keenly felt, and I well remember one time when this subject was the topic of conversation at the supper table, that he remarked to a gentleman present, "my position is not a pleasant one," and turning to me, repeated with emphasis, "no! it is *not* a pleasant one." The words seemed to come from the depths of a full heart, and I shall never forget their pathos and feeling. Altogether, Mr. Marwood never encouraged me in any way to think of his calling with feelings of envy, and though he did give me all particulars of his methods and apparatus, it was merely because I asked all sorts of questions from natural curiosity.

It was only when in company with Mr. Marwood, with whom I became quite friendly, that I ever contemplated the question of capital punishment. At other times it was far from my thoughts. My application for the post, which was left vacant at his death, was, therefore, in no way the result of a personal desire for the work or of a pre-conceived plan. I was simply driven to it by the poverty-stricken condition of my family, which I was unable to keep in reasonable comfort upon my earnings (I was then engaged as a boot-salesman, at a small salary). I knew that in the line on which I was then working there was no prospect of a material improvement in my position; I knew that I was a man of no extraordinary ability, so that my chances of rising were few, and I looked upon the vacancy of the executioner's post as being probably my one chance in life, my "tide in the affairs of men." Personally I had a great distaste for the work, though I did not consider it in any way dishonourable or degrading, and I had to weigh my family's wants against my personal inclination. It seemed to me at the time that my duty was clear, so I made application for the vacant position.

It may be said that I decided to better myself without any regard to the means of that betterment, or to my fitness for the position; but when I carefully considered the matter, in the few days before sending in my application, I was convinced that

I could do the work as well as anyone, and that I could make practical improvements in some of the methods and somewhat improve the lot of those appointed to die. This last consideration finally decided me.

I made application to the Sheriffs of London and Middlesex in September, 1883. There were some 1400 applicants for the post, but after waiting some time I received the following letter intimating that I was one of the few from amongst whom the final choice was to be made:——

London.

The Sheriffs of London and Middlesex will be at the Old Bailey on Monday next, the 24th instant, at 2 o'clock p.m., for the purpose of seeing the selected applicants for the post of Executioner. If you (as one of those selected for consideration) are disposed to attend at the above time and place you are at liberty, at your own expense, to do so.

19th September, 1883.
To Mr. J. Berry.

Of course, I kept the appointment, was duly examined, amongst some nineteen others, and was told that the chosen executioner would be communicated with.

My action in applying for the post was not at all in accordance with the wishes of my relatives, who did everything they possibly could to prevent my obtaining it. Some of my friends and neighbours wrote, either through solicitors or personally, to the sheriffs. Certain members of my own family petitioned the Home Secretary to dismiss the application, on the ground that if the appointment was given to me, a hitherto respectable family would be disgraced. I believe that it was mainly in consequence of these representations that I was passed over, and the post given to Mr. Bartholomew Binns. Upon myself the opposition had an effect that was not intended. It made me devote considerable thought and care to the details of the work of an executioner, and made me determine that if ever the opportunity again offered I should do my best to secure the work. During the four months that Mr. Binns held the appointment I had consultations with some eminent medical men, and when, much earlier than I expected, a new executioner was wanted, I was very well grounded in the theory of the subject. It was in March, 1884, that the magistrates of the city of Edinburgh wanted a man to execute Vickers and Innes, two poachers. The Sheriffs of London and Middlesex gave me a recommendation, and I addressed the following letter to the Magistrates of Edinburgh:—

March 13th, 1884.
52, Thorpe Street, Shearbridge,
Bradford, Yorkshire.

To the Magistrates
of the City of Edinburgh.

DEAR SIRS,

I beg most respectfully to apply to you, to ask if you will permit me to conduct the execution of the two Convicts now lying under sentence of death at Edinburgh. I was very intimate with the late Mr. Marwood, and he made me thoroughly acquainted with his system of carrying out his work, and also the information which he learnt from the Doctors of different Prisons which he had to visit to carry out the last sentence of the law. I have now one rope of his which I bought from him at Horncastle, and have had two made from it. I have also two Pinioning straps made from his, also two leg straps. I have seen Mr. Calcraft execute three convicts at Manchester 13 years ago, and should you think fit to give me the appointment I would endeavour to merit your patronage. I have served 8 years in

Bradford & West Riding Police Force, and resigned without a stain on my character, and could satisfy you as to my abilities and fitness for the appointment. You can apply to Mr. Jas. Withers, Chief Constable, Bradford, also to the High Sheriff for the City of London, Mr. Clarence Smith, Mansion House Buildings, 4, Queen Victoria Street, London, E.C., who will testify as to my character and fitness to carry out the Law. Should you require me I could be at your command at 24 hours' notice. Hoping these few lines will meet with your approval. I remain, Sirs,

> Your Most Obedient Servant,
> JAMES BERRY.

> To The Chief Magistrates,
> *Borough of Edinburgh,*
> *Scotland.*

> P.S. An answer would greatly oblige as I should take it as a favour.

A brief correspondence followed, and on March 21st I received the following letter from the Magistrates' Clerk:

> *City Chambers, Edinburgh,*
> *21st March, 1884.*

SIR,

With reference to your letters of the 13th and 15th instant, I am now directed by the Magistrates to inform you that they accept the offer you have made of your services to act as Executioner here on Monday, the 31st March current, on condition (1) that you bring your Assistant with you, and (2) that you and your Assistant arrive in Edinburgh on the morning of Friday the 28th instant, and reside within the Prison (at the

Magistrates' expense) till after the Executions are over.

The Magistrates agree to your terms of ten guineas for each person executed and 20s. for each person executed to your Assistant, with second-class railway fares for both of you, you finding all necessary requisites for the Executions.

> I am, Sir,
> Your obedient servant,
>
> A CAMPBELL,
> *Deputy City Clerk.*
>
> Mr. JAMES BERRY,
> 52, *Thorpe Street,*
> *Shearbridge,*
> *Bradford, Yorks.*
>
> P.S. Please acknowledge receipt of this letter immediately.—A. C.

Of course, my reply was to the effect that I accepted the engagement, and although I felt many misgivings between that time and the day appointed for the execution, the work was carried through satisfactorily.

Calton Gaol, from Calton Hill

CHAPTER III

MY FIRST EXECUTION[1]

IN the 21st March, 1884, I received a letter from the Magistrates' Clerk, City Chambers, Edinburgh, appointing me to act as Executioner on 31st March, 1884, at Calton Gaol; and that I was to provide all necessary appliances for carrying out the same. I undertook the duties; and on Thursday, March 27th, 1884, I departed from my home, Bradford, and made my way to the Midland Station, and booked 3rd class for Edinburgh, to carry out the execution of the Gorebridge murderers. I arrived at Waverley Station 4-20 p.m., and I hired a cab to drive me to the gaol. On arrival at the prison I was met at the doors by a good-looking warder, dressed in ordinary prison garb, and very courteous; and on entering the large portal gate, was asked my name, and after entering it down in the prison book, time, etc., he pulled a string, which rang the Governor's bell, and in a few moments I was confronted with the Governor, a very nice gentleman, of military appearance, and very good looking. After passing the usual conversation of the day, and the weather, and what kind of journey I had up from Bradford, he said after such a long journey I should require a good, substantial tea; and as soon as I had washed, and combed my hair, the tea was there, everything that could be desired. I sat down, and quite enjoyed my first Scotch meal in Bonnie Scotland . . .

[An examination of himself and his apparatus by the

---

1 This chapter is taken verbatim from Mr. Berry's note-book. Elisions are marked . . . —Ed.

Governor, and his own inspection of the scaffold, are then described at length.] . . . I returned to my room, and stayed in during the daytime. I spent the Thursday night smoking and reading. At 10-0 o'clock p.m. I was escorted to my bedroom, a round house at the back part of the gaol, about 40 yards from the back entrance, a snug little place, and was informed that the last man who slept inside that room was Wm. Marwood, five years previous to my visit. He was then there for the same purpose as myself, but the culprit in his case was a poisoner. The chief warder, whom I spoke to, seemed to touch upon the subject with great reluctance, and said that he felt quite upset concerning the two culprits, and that he hoped they would get a reprieve. I could see in his countenance a deep expression of grief, which was making him look no better for his occupation . . . I sat me down on my bed after he had gone, locked my door, and could hear the trains depart from the station under the prison wall. I looked out of my window at the mail taking its departure for the South . . . I then knelt down and asked the Almighty to help me in my most painful task, which I had undertaken to carry out . . . [The night was much disturbed by the persistent smoking of the chimney.] . . . At 8-0 a.m. on the morning of the 28th, Friday, my breakfast was brought into my room, consisting of toast, ham and eggs, and coffee . . . At 10-0 a.m. on Friday morning, 28th March, 1884, I was introduced to the Magistrates and those responsible to see the execution carried out. I exposed my ropes and straps for their inspection, and, after a long and careful investigation of all points, they retired, quite satisfied with their visit. After that we paid another visit to the scaffold; the builders, not having finished the contract, were making a final touch to the new-erected shed to keep the execution private, and so that nobody outside could see. After testing it with bags of cement, same weight as the prisoners, and calculating the length of drop and its consequences, and other details, the committee departed. After, I filled my time walking about the prison grounds, and thinking of the poor men who were nearing their end, full of life, and knowing the fatal hour, which made me quite ill to think about. My meals did not seem to do me good, my appetite began to fall off, nothing felt good to me, everything that I put into my mouth felt like sand, and I felt as I wished I had never undertaken such an awful calling. I regretted for a while, and then I thought the public would only think I had not the pluck, and I would not allow my feelings to overthrow me, so I never gave way to such thoughts again. At 1-0 p.m. my dinner had arrived. I went up to my room, and sat down to pudding, beef, and vegetables, Scotch broth, and Cochrane & Cantrell's ginger ale. At that time I was a total abstainer; and I think it is the safest side, since what I have seen brought on by its sad consequences of taking too much alcoholic liquor . . . After tea, I had a chat with the warders coming off duty for the day. As they passed through the wicket gate, one remarked, "He looks a nice fellow for a job like that;" another says, "But he has a wicked eye," and he would be sure I could do it . . . I was left smoking in the lodge with the gate-keeper and one (warder) who stayed behind to see what he could hear me say; but I looked him over, and could see by the look of his face that I was not to say much in his presence, as he was built that way . . . I was left alone with the gate-keeper, and he looked like a straight, honest man, and he was like myself. He said, "I am glad you never began to say anything in the presence of that man, as he would stop until morning." . . . Saturday morning, 29th . . . After breakfast, had another interview with the Magistrates, and made the final arrangements. I tested the scaffold in their presence, with the ropes I was going to use on the Monday morning, with bags of cement, each bag being placed in the same places as was marked for the criminals; Vickers, weighing 10 stones and over, 8 feet (drop); and Innes, 9 stones, 10 feet. One bag represented one, and the other bag the other. I tested the ropes by letting off the traps, and down went the bags, and I got my calculations from that point, after seeing the ropes tested with the weight of cement. They all looked quite satisfied with the results. The rope was of Italian silk hemp, made specially for the work, ⅝ inch in thickness, and very pliable, running through a brass thimble, which causes dislocation and a painless death if rightly adjusted . . . After dining, I had the honour of having a drive in an open carriage (provided by the Governor) for a couple of hours, . . . which I enjoyed, after being inside the prison gates since my arrival on Thursday . . . I gave my friend another night's visit at the lodge gate. We chatted on different topics of the day, and spent a nice, jovial evening together, smoking our weed; when a voice came to the door from a visitor from the offices of the town, that a reprieve was refused, and the law was to take its course, and I had a paper sent, with the words in full, Gorebridge Murderers, No Reprieve, which made me feel as bad as the condemned men for a time. But, what with the jolly gate-keeper, and another of the warders, I drove it out of my mind for a while . . . I retired to bed as usual at 10-0 p.m., after reciting my prayers, and thinking only another night and I shall be back with my wife and children. Saturday night I was very restless, and I did not feel so much refreshed for my night's sleep, as I was thinking of the poor creatures who was slumbering their hours away, in the prison cell, just beyond where I was laid, thinking of the dreadful fate that awaited them in such a short space of time. Two men, in full bloom, and had to come to such an untimely end, leaving wives and large families. One poor woman, I was informed, her mind was so affected that she was removed to the asylum, she took it so to heart . . . I retired to my day-room at the front entrance, where I only partook very sparingly of the nice and tempting ham and poached eggs put before me. I spent most of the forenoon looking round inside the prison, while the prisoners was at chapel, until dinner time. My dinner did not arrive until 4-0 o'clock, which is called late dinner, consisting of rice pudding, black currants, chicken, vegetables, potatoes, bread, and the usual teetotal beverages. I tried to make the best of it, but all that I could do was to look at it, as my appetite was gone; but I managed to eat a little before going to roost for the last night . . . I retired at 10-0 on Sunday, but only had cat naps all night, one eye shut and the other open, thinking and fancying things that never will be, and which is impossible. I was dressed and up at 5-0 a.m.; and felt more dead than alive as I had such a responsible part to play in the programme for the day. I fancied the ropes breaking; I fancied I was trembling, and could not do it; I fancied I fell sick just at the last push. I was nearly frantic in my mind, but I never let them know. 6-0 a.m. arrived. I heard the sound of the keys, clattering of doors, sliding of bolts. Breakfast had to be served earlier than usual. No prisoner allowed out of his cell until all was over. The public had begun to assemble on Calton Hill in groups. 7-0 a.m. arrived. I made my way to the scaffold, made my arrangements secure, and cleared the scaffold shed, the principal warder locking the door, not to be opened again until the procession enters for the great event of the day . . . At 7-45 the living group wended their way to the prison, and into the doctor's room, ready for the last scene of the drama. The prisoners were brought face to face for the first time since their conviction. They kissed each other; and the scene was a very painful one, to see mates going to meet their end on the gallows. They were conducted to the room adjoining the doctor's room, and were in prayer with the two ministers in attendance after 8-5. I was called to do my duty. I was handed the warrant, which was made out by the judge who condemned them to die. I then proceeded to pinion the prisoners, previously shaking hands, bidding good-bye to this world. Both men seemed to feel the position very much. The procession was formed, headed by the High Bailiff, the Chaplain reading the litany for the dead. Both the prisoners walked without assistance to place of execution; they was at once placed under the beam on the drop, where everything was done as quick as lightning, and both culprits paid the highest penalty of the law . . . The magistrates, and doctors, and even the pressmen, admitted that the execution of the two men had been carried out in an humane manner as possibly could be, and that the poor fellows had not suffered the slightest pain in going through the execution; doctors giving me a testimonial as to the skilful way I had carried out the execution. 9-0 a.m., my breakfast arrived; and I was so much affected by the sad sight I had witnessed, that I had no appetite, but just merely drank a cup of coffee; but eating was out of the question.

* * * * *

As this was my first execution, I was naturally anxious to have an assurance from my employers that it had been satisfactorily carried out. The magistrates, the governor, and the surgeons all signified their satisfaction, in the following terms:—

City Chambers, Edinburgh,
1st May, 1884.

We, the Magistrates who were charged with seeing the sentence of death carried into effect, on the 31st March last, on Robert F. Vickers and William Innes, in the Prison of Edinburgh, hereby certify that James Berry, of Bradford, who acted as Executioner, performed his duties in a thoroughly efficient manner; and that his conduct during the time he was here was in every way satisfactory.

GEORGE ROBERTS, *Magistrate.*
THOMAS CLARK, *Magistrate.*

H.M. Prison, *Edinburgh,*
31 March, 1884.

I hereby certify that Mr. James Berry, assisted by Mr. Richard Chester, carried out a double Execution in this Prison on this date, and that the whole of his arrangements were gone about in a most satisfactory and skilful manner; and, further, that the conduct of Messrs. Berry and Chester, during the four days that they resided here, has been all that could be desired.

J. E. Christie,
Governor of H.M. Prison.

Edinburgh, 31st March, 1884.

We hereby certify that we have this day witnessed the Execution of Vickers and Innes, and examined their bodies. We are of opinion that the Execution of these men was admirably managed; and that the Executioner Berry and his Assistant conducted themselves in a cool, business-like manner, to our entire satisfaction; death being instantaneous.

James A. Sidey, M.D.,
Surgeon to H.M. Prison of Edinburgh.

Henry D. Littlejohn, M.D.,
Surgeon of Police.

I fear it seems like self-praise to publish these "testimonials," but my work is so often maligned in common conversation, that I feel that it is a duty to give the opinions of a few of the men on the spot, who are most competent to judge of the matter. I believe that in every case where I have conducted an execution, the authorities have been perfectly satisfied, and I could produce numerous letters to that effect, but I will content myself with one, from the prison where I have had the greatest number of executions. It is dated a few years ago, but it would be endorsed now, and such testimony is very gratifying to me.

Strangeways Prison,
11th June, 1887.

During the period Mr. James Berry has been public Executioner he has always given satisfaction at this Prison in carrying out Capital Sentences, and his conduct has been marked by firmness and discretion.

J. H. PURTON, JR.

CHAPTER IV

MY METHOD OF EXECUTION

CALCULATIONS AND APPARATUS

MY method of execution is the outcome of the experience of my predecessors and myself, aided by suggestions from the doctors, and is rather the result of gradual growth than the invention of any one man.

THE DROP

The matter which requires the greatest attention in connection with an execution is the allowance of a suitable drop for each person executed, and the adjustment of this matter is not nearly so simple as an outsider would imagine.

It is, of course, necessary that the drop should be of sufficient length to cause instantaneous death, that is to say, to cause death by dislocation rather than by strangulation; and on the other hand, the drop must not be so great as to outwardly mutilate the victim. If all murderers who have to be hanged were of precisely the same weight and build it would be very easy to find out the most suitable length of drop, and always to give the same, but as a matter of fact they vary enormously.

In the earliest days of hanging it was the practice for the executioner to place his noose round the victim's neck, and then to haul upon the other end of the rope, which was passed through a ring on the scaffold pole until the culprit was strangled, without any drop at all. After a while the drop system was introduced, but the length of drop given was never more than three feet, so that death was still generally caused by strangulation, and not by dislocation, as it is at present. One after another, all our English executioners followed the same plan without thought of change or improvement, until Mr. Marwood took the appointment. He, as a humane man, carefully considered the subject, and came to the conclusion that the then existing method, though certain, was not so rapid or painless as it ought to be. In consequence he introduced his long-drop system with a fall of from seven to ten feet, which caused instantaneous death by severance of the spinal cord. I was slightly acquainted with Mr. Marwood before his death, and I had gained some particulars of his method from conversation with him; so that when I undertook my first execution, at Edinburgh, I naturally worked upon his lines. This first commission was to execute Robert Vickers and William Innes, two miners who were condemned to death for the murder of two game-keepers. The respective weights were 10 stone 4 lbs. and 9 stone 6 lbs., and I gave them drops of 8 ft. 6 in. and 10 ft. respectively. In both cases death was instantaneous, and the prison surgeon gave me a testimonial to the effect that the execution was satisfactory in every respect. Upon this experience I based a table of weights and drops. Taking a man of 14 stones as a basis, and giving him a drop of 8 ft., which is what I thought necessary, I calculated that every half-stone lighter weight would require a two inches longer drop, and the full table, as I entered it in my books at the time, stood as follows:—

14	stones	8	ft.	0	in.
13½	"	8	"	2	"
13	"	8	"	4	"
12½	"	8	"	6	"
12	"	8	"	8	"
11½	"	8	"	10	"
11	"	9	"	0	"
10½	"	9	"	2	"
10	"	9	"	4	"
9½	"	9	"	6	"
9	"	9	"	8	"

8½	"	9	"	10	"
8	"	10	"	0	"

This table I calculated for persons of what I might call "average" build, but it could not by any means be rigidly adhered to with safety. For instance, I have more than once had to execute persons who had attempted suicide by cutting their throats, or who had been otherwise wounded about the neck, and to prevent re-opening the wounds I have reduced the drop by nearly half. Again, in the case of persons of very fleshy build, who often have weak bones and muscles about the neck, I have reduced the drop by a quarter or half of the distance indicated by the table. If I had not done so, no doubt two or three of those whom I have executed would have had their heads entirely jerked off,—which did occur in one case to which I shall again refer. In the case of persons with scrofulous tendencies it is especially necessary that the fall should be unusually short, and in these cases I have at times received useful hints from the gaol doctors.

Until November 30th, 1885, I worked to the scale already given, but on that date I had the awful experience above referred to, which caused me to reconsider the whole subject and to construct a general table on what I believe to be a truly scientific basis. The experience referred to is dealt with in another chapter. The man with whom it occurred was Robert Goodale, whom I executed at Norwich Castle. He weighed 15 stones, and the drop indicated by the first table would therefore be 7 ft. 8 in., but in consequence of his appearance I reduced it to 5 ft. 9 in., because the muscles of his neck did not appear well developed and strong. But even this, as it turned out, was not short enough, and the result was one of the most horrible mishaps that I have ever had. As will be seen from the full report of this case, in another chapter, the coroner exonerated me from all blame and testified to the careful way in which I had done my work; but I felt that it was most necessary to take every possible precaution against the recurrence of such an affair. I, therefore, worked out a table of the striking force of falling bodies of various weights falling through different distances; which table I give on page 34. Working with this, I calculate that an "average" man, of any weight, requires a fall that will finish with a striking force of 24 cwt., and if the convict seems to require less, I mentally estimate the striking force that is necessary, and then by referring to the table I can instantly find the length of drop required. To see how this new table works out we may take the case of Robert Goodale again. As he weighed 15 stones his striking force with a drop of 2 feet would be 21 cwt. 21 lbs., or with a drop of 3 feet 26 cwt. 7 lbs., so that if he were a man of ordinary build the drop necessary would be 2 ft. 6 in. As I estimated from his appearance that his drop ought to have been about one-sixth less than the standard, I should have given him, working on this new table, about 2 ft. 1 in. instead of the 5 ft. 9 in. which was actually given. This is an extreme case, with a very heavy man, but all through the table it will be found that the drop works out shorter than in the first table. For instance, Vickers and Innes, the two Edinburgh murderers previously referred to would have had their drops reduced from 8 ft. 6 in. and 10 ft. to 5 ft. 6 in. and 7 ft. respectively if they had been treated according to the present revised table.

On August 20th, 1891, at Kirkdale Gaol, Liverpool, at the execution of John Conway, an attempt was made to dictate to me the length of drop, and a most unfortunate scene ensued. From seeing the convict, Conway, I had decided that the drop ought to be 4 ft. 6 in., a little under the scale rate; and I was surprised and annoyed at being told by Dr. Barr, acting, I believe, under authority, that I was to give a drop of 6 ft. 9 in. I said that it would pull the man's head off altogether, and finally refused to go on with the execution if such a long drop were given.

SCALE SHOWING THE STRIKING FORCE OF FALLING BODIES AT DIFFERENT DISTANCES.

Falling Distance in Feet	8 Stone (Cw. Qr. lb.)	9 Stone (Cw. Qr. lb.)	10 Stone (Cw. Qr. lb.)	11 Stone (Cw. Qr. lb.)	12 Stone (Cw. Qr. lb.)	13 Stone (Cw. Qr. lb.)	14 Stone (Cw. Qr. lb.)	15 Stone (Cw. Qr. lb.)	16 Stone (Cw. Qr. lb.)	17 Stone (Cw. Qr. lb.)	18 Stone (Cw. Qr. lb.)	19 Stone (Cw. Qr. lb.)
Zero	0 0 0	0 0 0	0 0 0	0 0 0	0 0 0	0 0 0	0 0 0	0 0 0	0 0 0	0 0 0	0 0 0	0 0 0
1 Ft.	11 1 15	12 2 23	14 0 14	15 2 2	16 3 22	18 1 12	19 3 2	21 0 21	22 2 11	24 0 1	25 1 19	26 3 9
2 "	13 3 16	15 2 15	17 1 14	19 0 12	20 3 11	22 2 9	24 1 8	26 0 7	27 3 5	29 2 4	31 1 2	33 0 1
3 "	16 0 0	18 0 0	20 0 0	22 0 0	24 0 0	26 0 0	28 0 0	30 0 0	32 0 0	34 0 0	36 0 0	40 0 0
4 "	17 2 11	19 3 5	22 0 0	24 0 22	26 1 16	28 2 11	30 3 5	33 0 0	35 0 22	37 0 16	39 2 11	41 3 15
5 "	19 2 11	22 0 5	24 2 2	26 3 22	29 1 16	31 3 11	34 1 5	36 3 0	39 0 22	41 2 16	44 0 11	46 2 5
6 "	21 0 22	23 3 11	26 2 2	29 0 16	31 3 5	34 1 22	37 0 11	39 3 0	42 1 16	45 0 5	47 2 22	50 1 11
7 "	22 2 22	25 2 4	28 1 14	31 0 23	34 0 5	36 3 15	39 2 25	42 2 7	45 1 16	48 0 26	51 0 8	53 3 18
8 "	24 0 11	27 0 12	30 0 14	33 0 23	36 0 16	39 0 18	42 0 19	45 0 21	48 0 22	51 0 23	54 0 25	57 0 26
9 "	25 1 5	28 1 23	31 2 14	34 3 4	37 3 22	41 0 12	44 1 2	47 1 21	50 2 11	53 3 1	56 3 19	60 0 9

35

Dr. Barr then measured off a shorter drop, some ten or twelve inches shorter, but still much longer than I thought necessary, and I reluctantly agreed to go on. The result, everyone knows. The drop was not so long as to absolutely pull off the victim's head, but it ruptured the principal blood-vessels of the neck.

I do not know who was really responsible for the interference with my calculation, but do not think that the long drop was Dr. Barr's own idea, as the drop which I suggested was on the same system as he had previously commended, and was almost identical with the drop that would have worked out on the basis of his own recommendation in a letter to the *Times* some years ago. Dr. Barr's letter to me, written in 1884, was as follows:—

1, *St. Domingo Grove,*
Everton, Liverpool,
Sept. 2nd, 1884.

Sir,

In compliance with your request I have pleasure in giving you a certificate as to the manner in which you conducted the execution of Peter Cassidy in H.M. Prison, Kirkdale. I may now report the statement which I gave in evidence at the Inquest, "that I had never seen an execution more satisfactorily performed." This was very gratifying to me.

Your rope was of excellent quality; fine, soft, pliable, and strong. You adjusted the ring, directed forwards in the manner in which I have recommended in my pamphlet, "Judicial Hanging." You gave a sufficient length of drop, considering the weight of the culprit, and completely dislocated the cervical vertebræ between the atlas and axis (first and second vertebræ). I have reckoned that the weight of the criminal, multiplied by the length of the drop, might range from 1120 to 1260 foot pounds, and I have calculated that this *vis viva* in the case of Cassidy amounted to 1140 foot pounds.

The pinioning and other details were carried out with due decorum, I hope, whoever be appointed to the post of public Executioner, may be prohibited from also performing the part of a "showman" to gratify a depraved and morbid public curiosity.

JAMES BARR, M.D.,
Medical Officer, H.M. Prison, Kirkdale.

To MR. JAMES BERRY.

A few days after Conway's execution I received a letter from a gentleman in the South of London, shortly followed by a second letter, and as they throw some useful light upon the subject I give them in full—omitting the writer's name, as he does not wish it to be published.

August 22nd, 1891.

Re THE EXECUTION AT KIRKDALE.

SIR,

As the accident attending the execution on the 20th inst. at Kirkdale may be falsely, and very unjustly, charged to your account, and at the same time be brought forward by a mass of misguided people as a reason for the total abolition of capital punishment, I think the following remarks on the subject of hanging may not be out of place.

Some years ago, Dr. James Barr, medical officer at Kirkdale Gaol, published a letter in the *Times* regarding what he considered the proper length of drop. He said that the length of drop ought to be such as to produce a momentum of 2600 lbs., meaning by "momentum," the convict's weight multiplied by the velocity of his descent at the end of the fall. Now, in estimating the convict's weight, I conceive that you ought to leave out the weight (as far as you can guess it) of his head, because the weight of his head is supported by the noose when the jerk takes place, and, therefore, cannot affect the amount of pull, or strain, on the neck. From what Dr. Barr says regarding the 2600 lbs. momentum, it is easy, by a little mathematics, to deduce the following rule.

To find length of drop in feet, divide the number 412 by the square of the convict's weight of body in stones.

By the above rule I constructed the following table:—

Weight of Body Without Head	Length of Drop
15 Stones	1 ft. 10 in.
14 Stones	2 ft. 2 in.
13 Stones	2 ft. 6 in.
12 Stones	2 ft. 11 in.
11 Stones	3 ft. 5 in.
10 Stones	4 ft. 2 in.
9 Stones	5 ft. 1 in.

8 Stones	6 ft. 6 in.
7 Stones	8 ft. 5 in.

Convict Conway's weight, you are reported to have said, was 11 stones 2 lbs. Leaving 1 stone for the weight of his head, which is perhaps more than sufficient, his hanging weight would be 10 stones 2 lbs, so that a drop of 4 feet and a few inches[2] would have been, according to the doctor's rule, quite enough for him. Regarding the value of the rule, I am, of course, unable to speak; nor do I know, from what I remember of the doctor's letter, that he meant the 2600 lbs. momentum to apply in all cases. Much depends on the convict's build, strength of neck, etc.

Yours truly,
X. Y.

(Second letter)

August 25th, 1891.

Re the Execution at Kirkdale.

Sir,

In constructing the table I sent you two days ago, I find that I have made an absurd mistake. It arose from my carelessly

2   The length of drop you, yourself, thought sufficient, as I read in the *Standard*.

taking a stone weight as 16 lbs., instead of 14 lbs., which I beg you to allow me correct. Instead of the number 412, I ought to have given the number 539. The corrected rule based on Dr. Barr's momentum of 2600 lbs. is, therefore, as follows:—Length of drop, in feet, is found by dividing the number 539 by the square of the number of stones in weight of convict's body, exclusive of the weight of his head. Thus, if a convict weighs 11 stones altogether, and we take his head as 1 stone, we have length of drop = 539/100 = 5·39 feet (5 ft. 5 in. nearly).

The table, corrected, stands thus:—

Weight of Body Without Head	Length of Drop
15 Stones	2 ft. 5 in.
14 Stones	2 ft. 9 in.
13 Stones	3 ft. 2 in.
12 Stones	3 ft. 9 in.
11 Stones	4 ft. 6 in.
10 Stones	5 ft. 5 in.
9 Stones	6 ft. 8 in.

8 Stones	8 ft. 3 in.
7 Stones	11 ft. 0 in.

In allowing, in the case of convict Conway, who weighed 11 stones 2 lbs., 1 stone for the head, I may be allowing too much; it is a mere guess. If his head weighed 9 lbs., the drop ought to have been 4 ft. 10 in.

Yours truly,
X. Y.

P.S.—A mistake of 3 or 4 lbs. in estimating weight of head makes, you will see, a considerable error in calculating the drop.

It will be seen that this calculation, which does not include the weight of the head in a man's hanging weight, works out the drop to a rather greater length than my own table, but the difference is only small, and I have always found my own table give quite sufficient drop.

THE ROPE

The apparatus for carrying out the extreme penalty of the law is very simple. The most important item is the rope, which must necessarily possess certain properties if the death of the condemned person is to be instantaneous and painless.

For successful working the rope must, of course, be strong, and it must also be pliable in order to tighten freely. It should be as thin as possible, consistent with strength, in order that the noose may be free running, but of course, it must not be so thin as to be liable to outwardly rupture the blood vessels of the neck.

Before undertaking my first execution I gave careful consideration to the question of the most suitable class of rope, and after trying and examining many varieties, I decided upon one which I still use. It is made of the finest Italian hemp, ¾ of an inch in thickness. Before using a rope for an execution, I thoroughly test it with bags of cement of about the weight of the condemned person, and this preliminary testing stretches the cord and at the same time reduces its diameter to ⅝ of an inch. The rope consists of 5 strands, each of which has a breaking strain of one ton dead weight, so that it would seem unnecessary to test it from any fear of its proving too weak, but the stretching and hardening which it undergoes in the testing makes it far more "fit" and satisfactory for its work than a new, unused rope would be.

It has been said that I use a rope with a wire strand down the centre, but the notion is so ridiculous that I should not refer to it if it were not that many people seem to believe it, and that more than once it has been stated in the newspapers. A rope with a wire strand would possess no possible advantage that I can see, and it would have so many practical disadvantages that I do not think anyone who had studied the matter would dream of using such a thing. At any rate I have not done so, and I know that neither Mr. Binns nor Mr. Marwood ever did. Mr. Marwood used ropes of about the same quality and thickness as my own, while Mr. Binns used a much thicker rope (about 1¼ inch diameter after use), of a rougher and less pliable class of hemp.

Until the commencement of 1890 I supplied my own ropes, some of which, however, were made to order of the Government, and I was able to use the same rope again and again. One I used for no less than sixteen executions, and five others I have used for twelve executions each. These are now in the possession of Madame Tussaud. At the beginning of 1890 a new rule was made under which a new rope is ordered to be supplied and used for most of the executions in England, and to be burned, together with the clothes of the person executed (which were formerly a perquisite of the executioner) by the prison officials immediately after the execution. In Scotland and Ireland I still provide my own ropes.

The rope I use is thirteen feet long and has a one-inch brass ring worked into one end, through which the other end of the rope is passed to form the noose. A leather washer which fits the rope pretty tightly, is used to slip up behind the brass ring, in order to prevent the noose slipping or slackening after it has been adjusted.

In using the rope I always adjust it with the ring just behind the left ear. This position I never alter, though of course, if there were any special reason for doing so, for instance, if the convict had attempted suicide and were wounded on the side of the throat, death could be caused by placing the ring under the chin or even behind the head. The position behind the ear, however, has distinct advantages and is the best calculated to cause instantaneous and painless death, because it acts in three different ways towards the same end. In the first place, it will cause death by strangulation, which was really the only cause of death in the old method of hanging, before the long drop was introduced. Secondly, it dislocates the vertebra, which is now the actual cause of death. And thirdly, if a third factor were necessary, it has a tendency to internally rupture the jugular vein, which in itself is sufficient to cause practically instantaneous death.

PINIONING STRAPS, ETC

The pinioning arrangement, like the rest of the arrangements for an execution, are very simple. A broad leathern body-belt is clasped round the convict's waist, and to this the arm-straps are fastened. Two straps, an inch and a half wide, with strong

43

steel buckles, clasp the elbows and fasten them to the body-belt, while another strap of the same strength goes round the wrists, and is fastened into the body-belt in front. The legs are pinioned by means of a single two-inch strap below the knees. The rest of the apparatus consists of a white cap, shaped somewhat like a bag, which pulls down over the eyes of the criminal to prevent his seeing the final preparations.

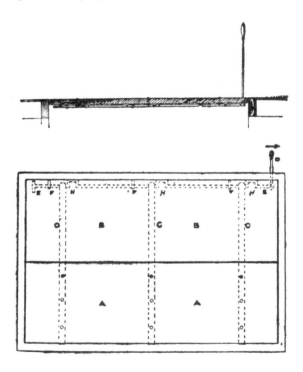

Plan and elevation of the Drop

THE SCAFFOLD

Until recently, the scaffolds in use in the various gaols differed very much in the details of their construction, as there was no official model, but in each case the local authorities followed their own idea. In 1885, however, a design was drawn, in the Surveyors' Department of the Home Office, by Lieut.-Col. Alten Beamish, R.E. Before being finally adopted, the design was submitted to me; and it seemed a thoroughly good one, as, indeed, it has since proved to be, in actual practice. The design is supplied to the authorities of any gaol where a scaffold is to be erected, from the Engineers' Department at the Home Office; and, with a slight alteration, has been the pattern in general use to the present day. The alteration of which I speak, is a little one suggested by myself, and consists of the substitution of a slope, or a level gangway, in place of the steps. I had found in some cases, when the criminals were nervous or prostrated, that the steps formed a practical difficulty. The slope, or gangway, was approved by the Home Office, and was first used on April 15th, 1890, at Kirkdale Gaol, for the execution of Wm. Chadwick. It was a simple improvement, but it has turned out to be a very useful one.

At most of the gaols in the country the scaffold is taken to pieces and laid away immediately after use, but in Newgate, Wandsworth, Liverpool, and Strangeways (Manchester), it is kept standing permanently.

The essential parts of the scaffold are few. There is a heavy cross-beam, into which bolts terminating in hooks are usually fastened. In some cases this cross-beam stands on two upright posts, but usually its ends are let into the walls of the scaffold house. Of course, the hooks fastened to it are intended to hold the rope.

The scaffold proper, or trap, or drop, as it is variously called, is the portion of the structure to which most importance is attached, and of which the Government furnishes a plan. It

45

consists of two massive oaken doors, fixed in an oak frame-
work on a level with the floor, and over a deep bricked pit. The
plan and section will explain the arrangement. The two doors
are marked A A and B B on the plan. The door A A is hung on
three strong hinges, marked C C C, which are continued under
the door B B. When the trap is set the ends of these long hinges
rest on a draw-bar E E, as shown in the plan. The draw-bar is of
iron, 1¼ in. square, sliding in strong iron staples, F F F, which
fit it exactly. When the lever D is pulled over in the direction of
the little arrow, it moves the draw-bar in the opposite direction,
so that the ends of the long hinges drop through the openings H
H H, and the two doors fall. To set the trap the door B B has to
be raised into a perpendicular position, until the other door is
raised and its hinges placed on the draw-bar. The arrangement
is a very good one; as both doors must necessarily fall at exactly
the same moment. Their great weight—for they are of three
inch oak—causes them to drop very suddenly, even without the
weight of the criminal, and they are caught by spring catches to
prevent any possibility of rebound.

Newgate

CHAPTER V

MY METHOD OF EXECUTION

THE PROCEEDINGS

THE hour fixed for executions is 8-0 a.m. in all the prisons, except Wandsworth and Lincoln, where it is 9-0 a.m. Of course, the scaffold and rope are arranged, and the drop decided, beforehand. I calculate for three minutes to be occupied from the time of entering the condemned cell to the finish of life's great tragedy for the doomed man, so I enter the cell punctually at three minutes to eight. In order that my action in hanging a man may be legal, it is necessary that I should have what is known as an "authority to hang," which is drawn up and signed by the Sheriff, and handed to me a few minutes before the time for the execution. Its form varies a good deal. In some cases it is a long, wordy document, full of the "wherefores" and "whatsoevers" in which the law delights. But usually it is a simple, official-looking form, engrossed by the gaol clerk, and running somewhat as follows:—

To JAMES BERRY.

I, ——, of ——, in the County of ——, Esquire, Sheriff of the said County of ——, do hereby authorise you to hang A—— B——, who now lies under Sentence of Death in Her Majesty's Prison at ——.

47

Dated this —— day of ——, ——.

—— ——, Sheriff.

This is folded in three, and endorsed outside.

Re A—— B——.

Authority to Hang.

—— ——, Sheriff,

——shire.

When we enter the condemned cell, the chaplain is already there, and has been for some time. Two attendants, who have watched through the convict's last nights on earth are also present. At my appearance the convict takes leave of his attendants, to whom he generally gives some little token or keepsake, and I at once proceed to pinion his arms.

As soon as the pinioning is done, a procession is formed, generally in the following order:—

Chief Warder.

Warder.   Warder.

Warder.   { Chaplain. / Convict. }   Warder.

Executioner.

Principal Warder.   Principal Warder.

Warder.   Warder.

Governor and Sheriff.

Wand Bearer.   Wand Bearer.

Gaol Surgeon and Attendant.

In some few cases, where the prisoner has not confessed before the time for the execution, I have approached him in the cell in a kindly manner, asking him, as it can make no difference to his fate, to confess the justice of the sentence, in order that I may feel sure that I am not hanging an innocent person. In most cases they have done so, either in the cell, or at the last moment on the scaffold. Of course, the confidences reposed in me at such moments I have never divulged, and it would be most improper to do so; but I am at liberty to state, that of all the people I have executed, only two or three have died without fully and freely confessing their guilt.

On the way from the cell to the scaffold the chaplain reads the service for the burial of the dead, and as the procession moves I place the white cap upon the head of the convict. Just as we reach the scaffold I pull the cap over his eyes. Then I place the convict under the beam, pinion the legs just below the knees, with a strap similar to the one used for the elbows, adjust the rope, pull the bolt and the trap falls. Death is instantaneous, but the body is left hanging for an hour, and is then lowered into a coffin, made in the prison, and carried to the mortuary to await the inquest. The inquest usually takes place at ten o'clock, but in some few places it is held at noon. After the inquest the body is surrounded by quick-lime and buried in the prison grounds.

In the carrying out of the last penalty of the law, everything is conducted with decorum and solemnity, and so far as I can see there is no way in which the arrangements at an execution can be improved, unless it is in regard to the admission of reporters. In years gone by a large number of reporters were often admitted, some of them with probably little or no real connection with the papers they professed to represent. Occasionally also there would be one or two feather-brained juniors who seemed to have no proper idea of the solemnity of a death scene, and whose conduct was hardly such as serious persons could approve. The result has been that in many prisons the admission of press representatives has been very rigidly curtailed, and in some cases admission has been absolutely refused. It seems to me that the admittance of a large number of spectators, and the absolute refusal to admit any, are alike mistakes. I speak in this matter as a man whose own work comes under the criticism of the press, and although so far as I am personally concerned, I am perfectly satisfied if I can satisfy the Governor or High Sheriff, I know that there is a large section of the public that thinks the exclusion of the reporters must mean that there is something going on which there is a desire to hush up. I am a servant of the public, as also are the sheriffs, the governor, and the other officials connected with an execution, and the public, through its representatives on the press, ought to have some assurance that the details of each execution are carried out decently and in order. The presence or absence of the press, of course, makes no difference in the conduct of the execution, but it makes a good deal of difference to a certain section of the public. If the Governor of the gaol or the Sheriff were to give three admissions for each execution, with the understanding that any representative suspected of not being *bona fide* would be refused admission even if he presented his ticket, I think that every real objection would be met.

After the execution is over the fact that the sentence of the law has been carried out is announced to the public by a notice fixed to the door of the prison. The form of this notice varies somewhat, but I append one of which I happen to have a copy.

COUNTY OF OXFORD.
EXECUTION of CHARLES SMITH for MURDER

(The Capital Punishment Amendment Act, 1868.)

Copies are subjoined of the official declaration that judgement of death has been executed; and of the Surgeon's certificate of the death of Charles Smith.

THOMAS M. DAVENPORT,
Under-Sheriff of the County of Oxford.
9th May, 1887.

OFFICIAL DECLARATION

We, the undersigned, do hereby declare that Judgement of Death was this day, in our presence, executed on Charles Smith, within the walls of Her Majesty's Prison at Oxford.

Dated this Ninth day of May, One thousand eight hundred and eighty-seven.

THOMAS M. DAVENPORT, *Under-Sheriff of Oxfordshire.*
H. B. ISAACSON, *Governor of the Prison.*
J. K. NEWTON, *Chaplain of the Prison.*
J. RIORDON, *Chief Warder of the Prison.*
HENRY IVES, *Sheriff's Officer.*
THOS. WM. AUSTIN, *Reporter, Oxford Journal.*
ROBERT BRAZIES, *Reporter, Oxford Chronicle.*
JOSEPH HENRY WARNER, *Reporter, Oxford Times.*
J. LANSBURY, *Warder.*

SURGICAL CERTIFICATE

I, Henry Banks Spencer, the Surgeon of Her Majesty's Prison at Oxford, hereby certify that I this day examined the body of Charles Smith, on whom judgement of death was this day executed in the said prison; and that, on such examination, I found that the said Charles Smith was dead.

Dated this Ninth day of May, One thousand eight hundred and eighty-seven.

HENRY B. SPENCER,
Surgeon of the Prison.

CHAPTER VI

OTHER METHODS OF EXECUTION

FROM time to time people raise an outcry against the English mode of putting criminals to death, and there are many Englishmen who have a firm conviction that hanging is the very worst and most unscientific form of capital punishment. The prejudices of these people seem to be based on an utterly wrong idea of how an English execution is conducted, and I hope that the chapter dealing with my method will form the basis for a truer judgment.

English Axe and Block, now in the Tower of London

Of methods of execution that have been suggested as substitutes for hanging, there are some which hardly deserve consideration, because there is no considerable number of people who would approve of them. The various methods of beheading are hardly likely to be ever in favour with Englishmen generally, for they want executions to be as free as possible from revolting details. The old headsman's axe and block which are still to be seen in the Tower, are in themselves sufficient argument against a revival of their use. Apart from the fact that beheading under the best conditions is revolting, we must further consider that from the very nature of the office, the executioner who has to hack off his victim's head must be a brutal and degraded man, and the chances are that he will not be so skilful or so careful as he ought to be for the performance of such a task. Even amongst races which are not so highly civilised as the English, and where it is easier to obtain headsmen of proportionately better standing, we occasionally hear of more than one blow being required to cause death, and such a state of things is very horrible. In China decapitation has been reduced to almost a science, and the Chinese executioners are probably the most skilful headsmen in the world. I have in my possession a Chinese executioner's knife, with which the heads of nine pirates were severed in nine successive blows, and a terrible knife it is, and well fitted for the purpose. Yet even with such a weapon, and with the skill and experience which Chinese executioners attain from frequent practice, the blow sometimes fails, as was the case in one of the last batch of Chinese executions reported in the English newspapers.

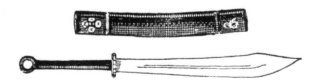

Executioner's Sword, Canton

Even the guillotine, which is often spoken of as the only perfect and certain method, has been known to fail, and we have cases in which the knife has been raised and dropped a second time before causing death. In any case, whether the guillotine, the axe, or the Chinese knife is used, and whatever care may be taken to render the death painless and instantaneous, there is a horrible mutilation of the sufferer that must be revolting to all sensitive people.

The Guillotine

The Spanish and Spanish-American method of execution, by means of the garotte, has been much praised by some advocates of reform. The prisoner to be garotted is placed in a chair, to the back of which an iron collar is attached in such a manner that it can be drawn partly through the chair-back by means of a heavily weighted lever. When the lever and weight are raised the head can be passed through the collar, and by dropping the weight the collar is drawn tight and causes strangulation. This method is certain, but I do not consider it so good as the present English system of hanging, because death by strangulation is much slower and more painful than death by dislocation. In one form of the garotting chair this fact has been recognised, and an iron spike is placed immediately behind the neck, so that when the pressure is applied the spike enters between two of the vertebræ and severs the spinal cord. This I consider worse than our own system, because the iron spike must cause a certain amount of bleeding, which the English method avoids.

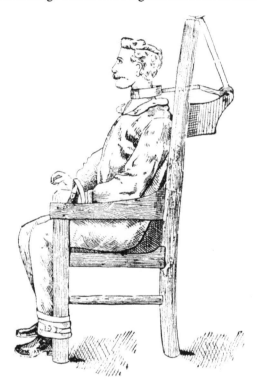

The Garotte

The American system of hanging, which has been recently superseded by electrocution, was but a slight modification of the ancient system of Jack Ketch, or the time-honoured method of Judge Lynch. In these older systems the convict stood upon the ground while the rope was placed round his neck, and the other end passed over the arm of the gallows, or the limb of a tree. Then the executioner and his assistants hauled on the other end of the rope, until the victim was swung clear off the ground and was gradually strangled. In the improved American method the place of the executioner was taken by a heavy weight which was attached to the rope and which rapidly ran up the convict to a height of some feet. In some few very extreme cases of heavy bodies with frail necks this may have caused dislocation, but as a rule strangulation would be the cause of death.

Old Methods

When the use of electricity for executions began to be talked of as a practical possibility, I naturally took much interest in the subject. As the result of all the enquiries I was enabled to make, I concluded that although electrocution—as the Americans call it—is theoretically perfect, it presents many practical difficulties. The experience of the authorities in the case of the wretched man, Kremmler, who was executed by electricity in New York, fully proves that as yet we do not know enough about the conditions under which electricity will cause painless and sudden death. When particulars of the method that was to be adopted for executions in New York were first published, I was with a small committee of gentlemen in Manchester who were investigating the subject. They made all arrangements for experiments to test the reliability of the method. Two animals were obtained that had to be killed in any case, namely, a calf and an old dog of a large breed. In the case of the calf the connections were made in the manner prescribed, and the current was turned on. This was repeated twice, but the only result was to cause the calf to drop on its knees and bellow with fear and pain, and the butcher at once killed it in the ordinary way with his poleaxe. When the shock was applied to the dog he fell down and seemed to be paralysed, but it was some time before life was extinct. The latest reports of American executions say that the deaths were instantaneous and painless, but the value of such statements is lessened by the fact of reporters being excluded. The total exclusion of the press at any rate seemed like an admission of the authorities that they had no confidence in the certainty of the method they were using.

Altogether, after a careful consideration of all the principal modes of execution, I am convinced that our English method as at present in use is the best yet known, because it is absolutely certain, instantaneous and painless.

It may be interesting to close this chapter with a list of the principal methods of execution in use in foreign countries.

Austria	Hanging, public.
Bavaria	Guillotine, private.
Belgium	Guillotine, public.
Brunswick	Axe, private.
China	Sword or bow-string, public.
Denmark	Guillotine, public.
France	Guillotine, nominally public; but really so surrounded by cordons of gens d'armes, &c., as to be virtually private.
Germany	Sword or hanging, private.
Hanover	Guillotine, private.
Italy	No capital punishment.
Netherlands	Hanging, public.

Portugal	Hanging, public.
Prussia	Sword, private.
Russia	Rifle shot, hanging or sword, public; but capital punishment is practically abolished except for political offences.
Spain	Garotte, public.
Switzerland	Fifteen cantons, sword, public. Two cantons, guillotine, public. Two cantons, guillotine, private.
United States	New York State, electric shock, private. Other states, hanging, private.

Wandsworth Gaol (after an execution)

CHAPTER VII

TWO TERRIBLE EXPERIENCES

THE whole of the duties of an executioner are unpleasant, but there are exceptional incidents occurring at times, which stand out upon the tablet of one's memory, and which can not be recalled without an involuntary shudder. I have had two of these experiences, and as people should always learn by their failures, have turned them to practical account as lessons for the future. The first was the attempted execution of John Lee, which resulted in the Home Office making an investigation into the arrangements for executions in the different gaols, and eventually to their issuing an official plan for the drop, which has been used in all prisons where scaffolds have since been erected. The second of these experiences was at the execution of Robert Goodale, when the length of the drop caused the head to be severed from the body. This taught me that the long-drop system then in use, and introduced by Mr. Marwood, was faulty in some cases, and caused me to work out my present table of lengths of drop, as explained in the chapter on "My Method of Execution."

There are so many erroneous ideas afloat about the details of these two cases that I think a good purpose may be served by giving the actual particulars, especially as no true explanation has ever been published of the difficulty which occurred in the case of Lee.

Lee was found guilty of the murder of Miss Keyse, in whose house at Babbacombe he was employed as a servant. Eight o'clock on Monday, February 23rd, 1885, was the time fixed for his execution. The scaffold and its arrangements had not been used for a previous execution, in their then position, though the drop had been used once, for the execution of Mrs. Took, but it was then fixed in another place. On the Saturday I examined this drop, and reported that it was much too frail for its purpose, but I worked the lever and found that the doors dropped all right. On the Monday morning, at the appointed time, I brought out the prisoner in the usual way, pinioned him and adjusted the noose. He was perfectly calm, almost indifferent. When the noose was adjusted I stood back and pulled over the lever. The noise of the bolts sliding could be plainly heard, but the doors did not fall. I stamped on the drop, to shake it loose, and so did some of the warders, but none of our efforts could stir it. Lee stood like a statue, making no sound or sign. As soon as we found our efforts useless we led the condemned man away. We tried the doors, which fell easily; then Lee was placed in position again, and again the doors refused to fall. Then the prisoner was taken away, and eventually his sentence was commuted. Perhaps it would be well to state here that the report to the effect that Lee has been since executed, and another report to the effect that he has been liberated, are both equally false; for he is still in prison.

Various reasons were given to account for the failure of the workings, but it was most generally believed that it was caused by the doors being swollen with the rain which fell on the Sunday night. That this was not the cause is proved, firstly, by the fact that the doors fell all right when the weight of the prisoner was not on them, and secondly, by the fact that they would not fall with the prisoner on them, even when we had chopped and planed down the sides where it was supposed that they stuck.

The Governor of the Gaol, and the Under-Sheriff, who were present, were terribly upset about the failure of the attempted execution, and the prolonged and terrible suspense in which the prisoner was kept. They were almost frantic about it, but nothing could be done in the matter.

The Under-Sheriff asked me to write out a brief statement of the facts, together with my opinion of the cause of the difficulty, and I give a copy of my letter below.

Executioner's Office,
1, *Bilton Place, City Road,*
Bradford, Yorks.,
4th March, 1885.

Re JOHN LEE.

SIR,

In accordance with the request contained in your letter of the 30th inst., I beg to say that on the morning of Friday, the 20th ult., I travelled from Bradford to Bristol, and on the morning of Saturday, the 21st, from Bristol to Exeter, arriving at Exeter at 11-50 a.m., when I walked direct to the County Gaol, signed my name in your Gaol Register Book at 12 o'clock exactly. I was shown to the Governor's office, and arranged with him that I would go and dine and return to the Gaol at 2-0. p.m. I accordingly left the Gaol, partook of dinner, and returned at 1-50 p.m., when I was shown to the bedroom allotted to me which was an officer's room in the new Hospital Ward. Shortly afterwards I made an inspection of the place of Execution. The execution was to take place in a Coach-house in which the Prison Van was usually kept. Two Warders accompanied me on the inspection. In the Coach-house I found a Beam about four inches thick, and about a foot in depth, was placed across the top of the Coach-house. Through this beam an iron bolt was fastened with an iron nut on the upper side, and to this bolt a wrought-iron rod was fixed, about three-quarters of a yard long with a hole at the lower end to which the rope was to be attached. Two Trap-doors were placed in the floor of the Coach-house, which is flagged with stone, and these doors cover a pit about 2 yards by 1½ yards across, and about 11 feet deep. On inspecting these doors I found they were only about an inch thick, but to have been constructed properly should have been three or four inches thick. The ironwork of the doors was of a frail kind, and much too weak for the purpose. There was a lever to these doors, and it was placed near the top of them. I pulled the lever and the doors dropped, the catches acting all right. I had the doors raised, and tried the lever a second time, when the catch again acted all right. The Governor was watching me through the window of his office and saw me try the doors. After the examination I went to him, explained how I found the doors, and suggested to him that for future executions new trap-doors should be made about three times as thick as those then fixed. I also suggested that a spring should be fixed in the Wall to hold the doors back when they fell, so that no rebounding occurred, and that the ironwork of the doors should be stronger. The Governor said he would see to these matters in future. I spent all the Sunday in the room allotted to me, and did not go outside the Gaol. I retired to bed about 9-45 that night. The execution was fixed to take place at eight o'clock on the morning of Monday the 23rd ultimo.

On the Monday morning I arose at 6-30, and was conducted from the Bedroom by a Warder, at 7-30, to the place of execution. Everything appeared to be as I had left it on the Saturday afternoon. I fixed the rope in my ordinary manner, and placed everything in readiness. I did not try the Trap-doors as they appeared to be just as I had left them. It had rained heavily during the nights of Saturday and Sunday. About four minutes to eight o'clock I was conducted by the Governor to the condemned Cell and introduced to John Lee. I proceeded at once to pinion him, which was done in the usual manner, and then gave a signal to the Governor that I was ready. The procession was formed, headed by the Governor, the Chief Warder, and the Chaplain followed by Lee. I walked behind

Lee and 6 or 8 warders came after me. On reaching the place of execution I found you were there with the Prison Surgeon. Lee was at once placed upon the trap-doors. I pinioned his legs, pulled down the white cap, adjusted the Rope, stepped on one side, and drew the lever—but the trap-door did not fall. I had previously stood upon the doors and thought they would fall quite easily. I unloosed the strap from his legs, took the rope from his neck, removed the White Cap, and took Lee away into an adjoining room until I made an examination of the doors. I worked the lever after Lee had been taken off, drew it, and the doors fell easily. With the assistance of the warders the doors were pulled up, and the lever drawn a second time, when the doors again fell easily. Lee was then brought from the adjoining room, placed in position, the cap and rope adjusted, but when I again pulled the lever it did not act, and in trying to force it the lever was slightly strained. Lee was then taken off a second time and conducted to the adjoining room.

It was suggested to me that the woodwork fitted too tightly in the centre of the doors, and one of the warders fetched an axe and another a plane. I again tried the lever but it did not act. A piece of wood was then sawn off one of the doors close to where the iron catches were, and by the aid of an iron crowbar the catches were knocked off, and the doors fell down. You then gave orders that the execution should not be proceeded with until you had communicated with the Home Secretary, and Lee was taken back to the Condemned Cell.

I am of opinion that the ironwork catches of the trap-doors were not strong enough for the purpose, that the woodwork of the doors should have been about three or four times as heavy, and with iron-work to correspond, so that when a man of Lee's weight was placed upon the doors the iron catches would not have become locked, as I feel sure they did on this occasion, but would respond readily.

So far as I am concerned, everything was performed in a careful manner, and had the iron and woodwork been

65

sufficiently strong, the execution would have been satisfactorily accomplished.

I am, Sir,

Your obedient Servant,
JAMES BERRY.

HENRY M. JAMES, *Esq.*,
Under-Sheriff of Devon,
The Close, Exeter.

The other miserable experience which lingers in my memory was, as before stated, the execution of Robert Goodale. He was condemned to death for the murder of his wife, and on November 30th, 1885, I was at Norwich Castle to conduct the execution. At that time I was working with my original table of lengths of drop, which I had based upon Mr. Marwood's system. This table, and some particulars of Goodale's case, or rather, of the new calculations which I made in consequence of the lesson then learned, will be found in the chapter on "My Method of Execution." He weighed fifteen stones, and the calculated drop for a man of that weight, according to the old table, was 7 ft. 8 in. As Goodale did not seem very muscular, I reduced the drop by about two feet—in fact, as closely as I could measure it, to 5 ft. 9 in. The rope that I used was one made and supplied by the Government, and I had used it seven days previously for the execution of John Williams, at Hereford. The drop was built on a plan supplied by the Government, and had been used before. In fact, everything was in perfect working order. The Governor of the gaol had been specially anxious that everything should be right, and had taken all possible precautions to avoid a hitch. He had personally tested the drop on the Thursday morning before, and on the Saturday had again tested it, in company with an engineer. The whole of the arrangements were carried out in the usual manner, and when I pulled the lever the drop fell properly, and the prisoner dropped out of sight. We were horrified, however, to see that the rope jerked upwards, and for an instant I thought that the noose had slipped from the culprit's head, or that the rope had broken. But it was worse than that, for the jerk had severed the head entirely from the body, and both had fallen together to the bottom of the pit. Of course, death was instantaneous, so that the poor fellow had not suffered in any way; but it was terrible to think that such a revolting thing should have occurred. We were all unnerved and shocked. The Governor, whose efforts to prevent any accident had kept his nerves at full strain, fairly broke down and wept.

The inquest was a trying ordeal for all concerned, and it was a great comfort to me to find that the Governor and the Gaol Surgeon both gave evidence as to the care with which every detail had been carried out. In the evidence I mentioned that I had hanged one heavier man previously, namely, Joseph Lawson, who weighed 16 stones 8 lbs., and to whom I gave a drop of 8 feet. In his case there was not even abrasion of the skin of the neck. When I finished my evidence the Coroner said:—"I am bound to say, before you leave the room, that as far as the evidence has gone there seems to be nothing to throw any blame upon you, either from want of skill or being in an improper condition." After this the evidence of the Gaol Surgeon was taken, and the jury returned a verdict to the effect that "Robert Goodale came to his death by hanging, according to the judgment of the law; and that no one was to blame for what had occurred."

In the foregoing I have spoken of *two* terrible experiences, and some of my readers, with the execution of Conway, at Kirkdale, fresh in their memories, will ask why it is not mentioned. The fact is, the foregoing was written before Conway's execution took place, and as the mishap which occurred on that occasion was in no way due to my own ignorance or carelessness, but was exactly what I expected would happen in consequence of my arrangements being interfered with by others, the shock that I received was by no means so great as on the two other occasions. Particulars of this execution will be found in the section headed, "The Drop," of the chapter on "My Method of Execution."

CHAPTER VIII

HOW MURDERERS DIE

AS one of my objects in writing this book is to give the public a solid basis for the formation of a sound public opinion upon the subject of capital punishment, it is necessary that the present chapter should be a long one, and that many of its details should be painful—because they are true. If I glossed over the facts I should signally fail in my duty to my readers, but I have endeavoured, so far as possible, to avoid revolting details.

To the ordinary Englishman a murderer is a murderer and nothing else. He is a vile creature who has taken life, and who by law, divine and national, must die because of his deed. He is a creature different from the rest of humanity, a fiend, a monster, who has outraged Justice, and must die like a dog. To me, a murderer is a study. He is a man who has done an ill deed, who may or may not be naturally vicious; who may or may not be really responsible for his actions; who may or may not be devoutly penitent. My own ideas on capital punishment are given in another chapter. I believe, honestly, and from long study of the subject, with unique opportunities of judging, that with a certain low class of the human brute, the fear of death is the only check that can in any way curb their lusts and passions. But I have sometimes thought that amongst those whom I have executed, for crimes which they have undoubtedly committed, there were men to whom their crime was a trouble more terrible than death; men who had not premeditated murder, who had taken no pleasure in it and expected no profit from it, and who, if they could by any means have been set at liberty, had within them the making of model citizens. Logically, and as a matter of conviction, I feel that if one sheddeth man's blood, by man should his blood be shed; but as a matter of sentiment, I sometimes feel sorry that certain murderers can not go free. The power of reprieve is, of course, often exercised, and very rightly so, and yet it sometimes seems as if murderers who have been wilful, deliberate and thoroughly vicious in their acts and characters are reprieved because they possess interesting personalities or influential friends, while others are executed who have a better plea for mercy, but no one to present it. The whole subject is a very difficult one; I must lay the facts before my readers and let them draw their own conclusions. But I may say that the executions which have given me the most trouble have not been those in which the convicts were violent or hysterical, not those in which they struggled and fought and cursed, or doggedly and stubbornly resisted; but the few cases in which they have been devoutly penitent, and almost seemed to welcome death as a release from a burden too heavy to be borne and an expiation for the sin which they deplored. In such cases the executioner's task is, indeed, a painful one.

The conduct of the condemned in the cell and on the scaffold throws much light upon the various phases of human character, and to me it has always been an interesting study.

ROBERT F. VICKERS AND WILLIAM INNES

The first two men whom I executed, though strong chums and partners in crime, were totally different from each other in their conduct. They both showed deep emotion, although they belonged to a low type of humanity, and they both attentively listened to the chaplain as often as he was willing to visit them, and to such outside ministers as took any interest in their fate, but I believe they did this with the view of making the best of a bad job—if any "best" were possible—rather than from any deep conviction of the sinfulness of their offence. Beyond this, their demeanour was totally different. Vickers was buoyed up with hope throughout, and continually asked if "the reprieve" had come. Even when I was introduced to him on the morning of the execution he had not despaired, and his hope rendered him almost cheerful. Even when we were on the scaffold he was convinced that he was not to die, and seemed to listen as people on the scaffold did in olden times, for the horseman wildly dashing across the court-yard and crying, "Reprieve! Reprieve!" at the very last moment. It was not until the noose touched his neck that he realised that his execution was to be an actual solemn fact, and when the dread reality burst upon him, he fainted.

His companion in crime and death stood unmoved upon the scaffold, resigned and calm, without either hope or fear. The white cap was over his face when Vickers fainted, and no sound from the bystanders gave him any hint that Vickers was overcome. The fainting man was supported for a moment, then a touch on the lever, and it was necessary to support him no longer. The Gorebridge murder, for which these men were executed, caused a great sensation at the time.

MARY LEFLEY

My next execution, in which the condemned person was a woman, was a very different experience. Mary Lefley, the culprit, was before her marriage a companion of Priscilla Biggadike, who was executed at Lincoln for poisoning her husband. Mary Lefley committed the same crime, poisoning her husband by inserting arsenic in a rice pudding. After the sentence of death, even up to the time of the execution, she expected a reprieve, and to the last she protested her innocence; though on the night before she was very restless and constantly exclaimed, "Lord! Thou knowest all," and prayed fervently. She would have no breakfast, and when I approached her she was in a nervous, agitated state, praying to God for salvation, not as a murderess but as an innocent woman. On my approach she threw up her hands and shrieked, "Murder! Murder!" and she had to be led to the scaffold by two female warders, shrieking wildly all the time. She died as she had lived, impenitent and untruthful, denying her guilt to the last.

Mary Lefley

JOSEPH LAWSON

The principal actor in the Butterknowle tragedy, when Sergeant Smith was murdered, was a terrible combination of craven fear and reckless bravado. During the last few days of his life he was dull and despondent, and during the night before his execution his sleep was frequently broken by fits of terror and nervous exhaustion, when he shivered like one in an ague. On the morning of the last day he arose at six o'clock, and tried to appear cheerful or even jovial. In the pinioning-room he saluted the warders with a cheerful "good morning," and on his way to the scaffold laughed hilariously at a stumble of his own. Then he commenced using foul, blasphemous language, and not ceasing even when the white cap was drawn over his face. His oaths drowned the voice of the chaplain who was reading the usual burial service, and with awful words on his lips he was launched into a dark eternity.

PETER CASSIDY

My very next case was a strong contrast to the foregoing. The condemned man was Peter Cassidy; his offence, wife-murder. It was one of those cases in which it is difficult to know whether the man should be most pitied or blamed, whether he was not more sinned against than sinning. That he committed the murder, in a fit of drunken frenzy, was undoubted—he did not deny it; but that he had received great and frequent provocation is certain. Both he and his wife were addicted to drink—which was most to blame for it I do not know—but on the day of the murder his wife was away from home for some time without his consent or knowledge of her whereabouts. When she returned she was drunk, so was he, and in the quarrel that ensued he slew her. But when he was sober again, his remorse was as deep as his drunken passion had been violent. He realised the gravity of his offence and the justice of his death sentence. To the ministrations of the Rev. Father Bonté, the Roman Catholic chaplain, he paid great attention, and on his last day on earth he seemed peaceful and resigned. He walked to the scaffold with a free, firm stride. The morning was dark and gloomy, but just as we passed across the prison yard a thin bright gleam of sunlight pierced the leaden clouds and rested for a moment upon the little procession. In that moment of sunshine Cassidy breathed convulsively, but the sky clouded over almost instantly and he regained his composure. On the scaffold he entered into the Roman Catholic service, which Father Bonté was reading, repeating the responses firmly and fervently, in fact, he was so engrossed in the service that I do not think he knew that I pinioned his legs. He continued his prayers as I adjusted the white cap over his eyes, but when the rope touched his neck he blushed crimson to the very roots of his hair, and his lips twitched. Intense shame and sorrow were never more plainly expressed by any man. A very large proportion of murders are directly traceable to drink, and in almost every case where a murderer has said anything about the motive for his crime he has blamed the drinking habit.

Moses Shrimpton

MOSES SHRIMPTON

As a rule, it is the first offender—there are many murderers whose great crime is their first offence—who is most affected by the terrible nature of his position when condemned to death. The old and practised criminal, though he has a great dread of the scaffold and the rope so long as he is at large, and though he usually takes more interest in his trial and uses greater efforts for his acquittal than the novice in crime, is usually resigned and indifferent as soon as the sentence is passed. As a rule, he pays but little heed to the ministrations of the chaplain, or the condolences of his friends. He is neither piously inclined, nor hysterically fearful, nor abusively rebellious—he simply waits his fate. A kind of hard stoicism seems to keep him quiet; he has played a desperate game with his eyes open, has played for high stakes—and lost. I say that this is generally the case with the gaol-bird; and yet there are exceptions, and amongst such exceptions in my own experience, Moses Shrimpton was notable. His life, almost from the cradle to the grave, was one long career of crime and punishment. He was a man of strong character and much determination of purpose, a leader amongst the ruffians of his district. He was sentenced to one month's imprisonment for poaching in February, 1848, and from that time until his execution in May, 1885, he was seldom out of prison for many months together. He gloried in his success as a poacher, and told the tales of his desperate adventures in a most interesting manner to the warders in Worcester Gaol, where he was a well-known and frequent inmate. He was sentenced to death for the violent and brutal murder of a policeman, who arrested him red-handed when fowl-stealing. He expressed no surprise or sentiment of any kind when he found that he was condemned to death, but to the astonishment of all who knew him, he appeared to be entirely changed in character by the thought of death. Those who administered spiritual consolation to him during his last three weeks of life were persuaded that his repentance and amendment were real, and certainly his actions appeared like those of a man who was really convinced. He paid great attention to the chaplain who visited him, and he read the Bible hour after hour. Certain passages that puzzled him he carefully noted down, and asked for an explanation at the chaplain's next visit. When the time for his execution came he was confident, almost defiant, and walked to the scaffold erect and firm. As he stepped on to the drop he glanced downwards and drew his feet together to assist me in fixing the strap that pinioned his legs. Before I pulled down the white cap he looked around as if to see the last of the world, and then, nodding to signify that he was ready, awaited the adjusting of the noose.

RUDGE, MARTIN AND BAKER

Some more ordinary examples of the deaths of hardened criminals were presented in the cases of Rudge, Martin and Baker. It will be remembered that these men committed a jewel robbery at Netherby, in Cumberland, and afterwards murdered police-constable Byrnes and made a murderous attack on other policemen, while endeavouring to escape arrest. These men, when once their sentence was passed, had no further interest in life; and I believe that if the choice could have been offered to them they would have preferred to walk straight from the dock to the scaffold, rather than to have had the three weeks' grace which is given to condemned men. In the case of almost all habitual criminals I believe this is so—they do not fear death and they do not repent of their crime. So long as there is a ghost of a chance of acquittal or reprieve, they cling to life, but as soon as the death sentence is passed they become indifferent, and would like to "get it over" as soon as possible, mainly because the prison life bores them.

Of the three men I have instanced, Rudge was the only one who seemed to care to take any interest in life. He spent a good deal of his time in writing a statement of his views upon the present system of penal servitude, for the information of the Home Office. As he had undergone two long sentences he knew his subject thoroughly from the inside. With his attendants he talked freely, both about himself and about other matters of interest. He insisted that there was something wrong with his head, which had caused him trouble several times in his life. He did not ask for any reprieve on this account, but he begged the prison chaplain to examine his brain after death, and repeated the request almost the last thing before the time for the execution. Martin and Baker spent most of the three weeks in bed. They would neither talk nor do anything else. Rudge and Martin were baptised Roman Catholics, whilst Baker had received some Protestant education, but none of them seemed to care for the ministrations of the priest or the gaol chaplain. To them it seemed cowardly and unreasonable to ask God for mercy simply because they were condemned to death, when they knew very well that they would have been living in defiance of God and man if they had remained free. After some time they yielded to the counsel and entreaties of their spiritual advisers so far as to listen to all they had to say. Baker appeared to attend carefully to the chaplain's ministration, and partook of Holy Communion an hour before the execution. Baker was troubled about the welfare of his sweetheart, Nellie, and spent part of the night before his execution in writing a long letter to her. In this letter he assured her of his love and constancy, and begged her to keep in the path of right.

All the three men walked firmly to the scaffold, where they shook hands all round, saying, "Good-bye, old pal, good-bye"—nothing more. The drop was already chalked with their names—Martin in the centre, with Rudge on the right and Baker on the left. The men stepped at once to their places and gave all the assistance they could in the final pinioning and in the adjustment of the nooses. Just before the drop fell Baker cried, "Keep straight, Nellie!" and then the three men died together, without a word of fear or even a quiver or a pallid cheek amongst them. The youth and manly bearing of Baker, and the strong affection of which he was capable, as shown by the way in which his Nellie was always uppermost in his thoughts, affected me very much. His execution was one of the saddest of my many experiences.

Mrs. Britland

MARY ANN BRITLAND

I have said that the people who are most cruel and callous in their murderous deeds are often most cowardly after conviction. The class of cruel and callous murderers is quite distinct from that of the violent murderers, like Rudge, Martin and Baker. These men, fighting against the law, fight fairly according to their lights. They take risks and meet the consequences in a straightforward manner. But the cruel and callous class show a cowardice and selfishness of which Rudge, Martin, and Baker were incapable. An instance of this occurs to me in the case of Mary Ann Britland, whom I executed at Strangeways Gaol,

Manchester. She was an example of the class of persons to whom the three weeks' respite before death is the greatest possible cruelty. She was condemned for the murder of a woman who had befriended her, and in whose house she was living as a guest at the time of the murder. She was also proved to have murdered her own husband and daughter by the same means, namely, poison. It seems hard to conceive of any adequate motive for such a series of crimes, extending over a considerable time, but a theory was advanced, and supported by her confession, to the effect that she desired to marry the husband of her latest victim. To accomplish this object she first killed her daughter (for what exact reason is not clear, unless she feared that the girl had some suspicion of her design upon the others), then her husband, and finally her friend, who had pitied her lonely and widowed circumstances, and given her food and shelter. The husband of the third victim was tried, with a view to bringing him in as an accomplice, but the investigation showed that he had never shown any friendliness for Mrs. Britland, and that it was clearly impossible that he could have had any connection with the murders. At her trial she was completely unnerved, not by remorse, but by fear. When the verdict was announced, and she was asked if she had anything to say why sentence should not be passed, she burst into tears. During the passing of the sentence she incessantly interrupted the judge with cries for mercy, but finding such appeals of no avail, she screamed to Heaven in tones of the greatest agony. Even after she had been removed to the cells, her screams could be heard for a long time by people outside. During the time that elapsed before her execution she was partly buoyed up by the hope of a reprieve, and protested her innocence almost to the very last. In spite of her hope, she could not shut out the terrible fear that the reprieve might not come, and the dread of death was so heavy upon her as to reduce her in three weeks to a haggard wreck of her former self. She prayed long and apparently earnestly for God's help, but did not acknowledge her guilt until almost the last moment, when she saw that there was no hope of reprieve. When the morning of the execution came, she was so weakened as to be utterly unable to support herself, and she had to be practically carried to the scaffold by two female warders. For an hour before the time of the execution she had been moaning and crying most dismally, and when I entered her cell she commenced to shriek and call aloud. All the way to the scaffold her cries were heart-rending, though her voice was weak through suffering, and as the white cap was placed over her head she uttered cries which one of the reporters described as "such as one might expect at the actual separation of body and spirit through mortal terror." The female warders held her on the drop until the noose was fixed, then their places were taken by two male warders who stepped quickly back at a signal which I gave them, and before she had time to sway sideways or to collapse the drop fell and the wretched woman was dead.

James Murphy

JAMES MURPHY

Some condemned persons are unconsciously humorous, whilst others that I have met with have shown an unconcerned and designedly humorous disposition, which is surprising when one considers the grave nature of my business with them. James Murphy, whom I executed at York, in November of 1886, for the murder of police-constable Austwick, of Barnsley, seemed to look upon his sentence and death rather as a joke than otherwise, and perhaps partly as a matter of pride. He never seemed to think that it was a very serious matter, and the principal reference that he made to the subject was a frequent assurance to his attendants that he would die firmly and show no fear on the scaffold. I was introduced to him by the Governor of York Castle the day before the execution, while he was at dinner. He was told that "a gentleman from Bradford" had come to see him, but he feigned not to understand my identity, and muttered, "Bradford! Bradford!—I have no friends at Bradford." Then it was explained that the gentleman in question was his executioner, and he smilingly replied, "Oh! of course!" but continued picking the mutton bone on which he had been engaged when we entered. In the last letter that he wrote, speaking of this incident, he said:—"I am in good spirits the Governor brought your letter to me at dinner time and the hangs man with him. I shaked hands with the hangs man and he ast me to forgive him and I did so. *But I eat my dinner none the worse for that.*" The same statement might also apply to his supper, and his breakfast next morning, for during the whole of his imprisonment his good humour and resolution never deserted him for a moment. He was perfectly contented with the arrangements made for him by the prison authorities; but the Roman Catholic priests in attendance could get no satisfaction out of him whatever. He parted from his brother, wife, and daughter without any sign of emotion, in the light-hearted manner of a working man who was starting for his day's labour. He did justice to his last meal,

81

and when it was finished asked for a "pipe of bacca," the only request that he made with which the Governor was unable to comply. He seemed to take a great interest in the pinioning process, and helped me as well as he could. His request was that I would execute him quickly and painlessly, and this favour I was able to grant.

EDWARD PRITCHARD

was hanged in Gloucester Prison on February 17th, 1887, for the murder of a boy at Stroud. The object was robbery, for the boy was carrying money to pay wages, from the bank. Pritchard practically pleaded guilty, and appeared to be sincerely sorry for his deed. He was not anxious to escape death, but took great pains to secure the forgiveness of the firm whose money he had taken, and of the parents of the boy whom he had murdered in order to get it. To the father of the lad he wrote a letter, earnestly begging for his forgiveness; and Mr. Allen, who was a good, kind-hearted man, journeyed to Gloucester to convey an assurance of that forgiveness in person, and to pray with the murderer. Owing to a prison regulation Pritchard was unable to receive Mr. Allen's visit, but the fact that the visit was made seemed a great consolation to the prisoner. While waiting for execution Pritchard frequently showed much emotion and it was feared that there might be a "scene" at the last moment, but when the time came, he was composed. There was no reckless bravado, but a quiet submission. He walked uprightly to the scaffold and stood motionless upon the drop. For a second his glance wandered round the prison-yard, and in that second he seemed to comprehend everything. He saw his grave, ready dug, in a corner, and heaved a sob, but this was his only demonstration of feeling whilst in my hands.

Walter Wood

WALTER WOOD

Another man who was apparently truly penitent was Walter Wood, executed at Strangeways, Manchester, on June 30th, 1887, for the murder of his wife. When the sentence of death was pronounced he was calm, and so he remained up to the time of execution. He did not falter even when visited by his mother and his two sons. He neglected no means of showing his contrition and making his peace with God, and on the day before his execution he attended the prison chapel, occupying a screened pew, where he paid careful attention to the service and appeared much solaced by a portion of the sermon which was introduced for his special benefit. On the morning of his last day he was awake early and spent the time with the good chaplain of the gaol. As I entered the cell the poor fellow was slowly repeating the responses to the prayers read by the chaplain, and

83

he continued to do so during the pinioning. The chaplain was assiduous in his attentions and did not weary of his good work even when on the scaffold, but continued to comfort and solace the doomed man with an earnestness that indicated the depth of his sympathy. At the last moment the calm, but wretched, culprit raised his head, drew a deep breath, and said in a deep, solemn, unshaken tone, "Lord have mercy upon me. Lord receive me." And so he died. This execution affected me deeply. The man was fully conscious of the hideousness of his crime, and sincerely repented. He assured the chaplain that he beheld the world and all things in a totally new light, and that the consciousness of his crime had changed his whole character. What would have been the fate of such a man if he could have been allowed to go free.

Alfred Sowrey

ALFRED SOWREY

One of the worst cases I ever had to deal with was that of Alfred Sowrey, hanged at Lancaster Castle on August 1st, 1887, for shooting the girl to whom he was engaged to be married, at Preston. He was impenitent, violent, and half-dead with fear by the day of execution. At the time of his trial he glared about in such a mad way that those who stood near the dock feared for their personal safety. During the time between sentence and execution he became seriously ill through sheer terror, and it was thought that he could not possibly live to the day appointed for his execution. The efforts of the gaol chaplain to bring Sowrey to a calmer and more reasonable state of mind seemed utterly unavailing, the prisoner was too terrified to take much notice of anything that was said to him. On the morning of the execution he took his breakfast as usual, but rejected the chaplain's ministrations. From the cell to the scaffold he had to be partly pushed and partly carried by two warders, in whose strong arms he struggled violently. His groans and cries could be heard all over the prison. His teeth chattered, and his face was alternately livid and deathly white. Every inch of ground over which the procession passed was violently contested by the criminal, who had to be bodily carried up the steps and placed on the drop. As he saw the beam above him a wilder paroxysm of fear seemed to seize the miserable youth, and four warders were required to hold him in position. Even with this assistance I had the greatest possible difficulty in pinioning his legs, and while doing so I received a nasty kick which took a piece of bone out of my shin, and has left a mark visible even to-day. After the completion of the pinioning process he still resisted the placing of the noose, throwing his head violently from side to side, and he continued his struggles until the drop fell. During the whole of this terrible scene the chaplain, who had taken much interest in his ungrateful charge, and who had done everything he could for Sowrey, continued reading the

85

beautiful prayers for the dying; but Sowrey paid no heed.

Dr. Cross

DR. PHILIP HENRY EUSTACE CROSS

My first execution in 1888 was that of Dr. Philip Henry Eustace Cross, who poisoned his wife by slow degrees, administering doses almost daily for a long time. Dr. Cross was a retired army surgeon, of good family. His medical experience gave him a great advantage in the commission of his crime, and he was evidently convinced that there was not the slightest fear of discovery. After conviction he protested his innocence until he received the message to the effect that there would be no

86

reprieve but that the law must take its course. He then relapsed into a mournful condition, and turned his attention entirely to the Bible. The last few days before his execution he was greatly prostrated, and on his last night of life he did not retire to bed until twelve o'clock. His sleep was restless and fitful. In the morning, however, he was resolute. He told his attendants that he did not fear death, for he had met it face to face more than once on the battlefield. He died unmoved, without a word.

JOSEPH WALKER

A sorrow-stricken face that often haunts me is that of Joseph Walker, executed at Oxford in November, 1887. He had murdered his second wife, after great provocation. Her reckless drinking habits and jealous disposition, developed soon after the marriage, had made the home absolutely miserable. On several occasions she threatened her husband with a knife, and the only way in which he could defend himself without injuring her was by seizing her wrists and holding her down on the floor until her fury abated. The climax was reached when one of Walker's sons by his first wife, who had been driven from home by his step-mother, committed suicide. The father attributed this to the step-mother's cruelty. She went to Croydon, where the suicide was committed, to attend the inquest, and instead of returning home remained in London until her husband went to fetch her. Up to this time he had been steady, but after the return from London he gave way to excessive drinking and neglected his work. On the day of the murder there was a violent quarrel between the man and his wife, and when he fell into a drunken sleep she rifled his pockets of a considerable sum of money. At night Walker cut his wife's throat, killing her with one terrible blow, and then, sobered by his act, called a neighbour to witness what he had done, and surrendered to the police who had been fetched to the house. The verdict of "Guilty" was brought in by the jury, but a strong recommendation to mercy was at the same time handed to the judge. In consequence of the great provocation which had been received by Walker, strenuous efforts were made to induce the Home Secretary to commute the death sentence to one of penal servitude, but without avail. The condemned man was perfectly willing to die, and his earnest repentance greatly touched the chaplain who laboured early and late to comfort him. Walker spent much of his time in fervent prayer, not for himself, but for his children. He prayed continuously that his sin might not be visited on them, for he knew how our Christian country usually treats those who have the burden of a dishonoured name to bear. He besought both God and man to treat his children kindly, and to lead them in the way of sobriety and honesty. For himself, while confessing the murder, he denied any premeditation of the matter. At the time of execution he was perfectly composed, and walked calmly to the scaffold, but he seemed to see nothing—his thoughts were far away—and even after death his face wore the same expression of sad composure. Walker was a heavy man, weighing over sixteen stones, and received a drop of 2 ft. 10 in., the shortest I have ever given.

JOHN JACKSON

Whose daring murder of warder Webb and escape from Strangeways Gaol, as well as his success in hiding from the police, caused immense interest to be taken in his case, was executed by me in the same gaol in which his crime occurred. Although he was commonly supposed to be incapable of feeling, his emotion at the prospect of his own fate was so touching that the official who had to tell him that reprieve was refused was very loth to break the news. On hearing it, he bowed his head and burst into tears, for, strange as it may seem, he had hoped that the death sentence would not be carried out. His grief continued to the last, and to the last he maintained that he had only intended to stun, and not to kill the warder. On the night before his death he did not sleep two hours, and when I entered his cell in the morning he was engaged in fervent prayer. He shook hands with me in a manner that was most affecting, and submitted quietly to the pinioning. He walked resignedly to the scaffold, and died without uttering a sound.

John Jackson

CHARLES JOSEPH DOBELL
AND WILLIAM GOWER

One naturally expects a hard indifference from an old criminal, but it saddens me to see it in the young, and yet two of the youngest men—or rather, boys—that I have executed were callous to the last degree. They were Charles Joseph Dobell (aged

17) and William Gower (18), executed in Maidstone Gaol for the murder of a time-keeper at a saw-mill in Tunbridge Wells some six months before. So carefully was the crime committed that the police could obtain no clue, and it was only found out by the confession of the lads to a Salvation Army officer. There is reason to believe that the lads' natural taste for adventure had been morbidly stimulated by the reading of highly sensational literature—"penny dreadfuls" and the like. They seem to have conducted themselves with a sort of bravado or courage which, if genuine, would have done credit to a patriot or martyr sacrificing himself for country or for faith, or to one of their backwoods heroes fighting against "a horde of painted savages," but which was distressing in two lads, almost children, sentenced to death for their crime. After they were sentenced they paid careful attention to the chaplain's words, but they showed no sign of emotion, and it was said that "it is doubtful whether at any time they fully realised the serious nature of their position." They walked to the scaffold in defiant manner, more upright than was their wont, and neither of them looked at or spoke to the other. There was no farewell, no word of repentance or regret, merely a brief supplication to God to receive them.

SAMUEL AND JOSEPH BOSWELL

It is a terrible trial to have to execute men who firmly believe, and apparently on reasonable, even if not correct grounds, that they are suffering an injustice. The worst instance that I remember of this kind was in the case of Samuel and Joseph Boswell, executed in Worcester Gaol for the murder of a game-keeper on the estate of the Duc d'Aumale, at Evesham. Three men, the Boswells and Alfred Hill, were found guilty of the murder, and the only difference which the jury could find in their guilt was that Hill was, if anything, the worst of the three. An application for a reprieve was made, apparently on the ground that though the men were guilty of poaching, they had not intended to commit murder. The Home Secretary responded to this application by reducing the penalty in Hill's case to penal servitude for life. This action fairly astounded the people of Evesham, who thought that there was no possible reason for making any difference in the fate of the three culprits. The Vicar telegraphed to the Home Secretary that his decision was "absolutely incomprehensible;" the Mayor, on behalf of the borough, telegraphed to the effect that "universal indignation" was "expressed by the whole community in Evesham and by county gentlemen." Several other similar messages were sent from other bodies, and the Vicar of Evesham was dispatched to London to interview the Home Secretary. The news was communicated to Hill but not to the Boswells, and as the feeling amongst outsiders was so strong, it can be imagined that the two men who had to suffer the punishment were shocked with a sense of injustice when they met on the morning of the execution and found that Hill had been reprieved. When they met on that fatal morning the brothers kissed each other, and, looking round, they enquired simultaneously, "where's Hill?" On being answered, they seemed utterly broken down with the feeling of the injustice of the arrangement. They asserted that Hill was the real murderer, whilst they were only accomplices. The men had been much troubled during their imprisonment by the thought of what would happen to their wives and children, and were in a terribly harassed and nervous condition. I put the white caps on their heads before leaving the cells, and a few steps from the door of the house in which the scaffold stood I pulled the caps over their eyes. This I always do when men are not quite firm and determined, before they see the scaffold. In the case of Samuel Boswell this simple act caused him to fall back into the arms of one of the warders in a state of collapse, and he had to be almost carried on to the scaffold. He moaned several times, until he heard his brother's voice give the response, "Lord, have mercy upon us," when he again drew himself together and answered,

"Christ, have mercy upon us." Then Joseph piteously cried, "Oh, my poor, dear wife," "Yes," answered Samuel, "and my dear wife and my poor children." Joseph turned his head a little and said, "Good-bye, Sam," to which his brother answered, "Good-bye, God bless you, Joe boy. Oh! dear, dear," Joseph continued: "I hope everybody will do well," and as he finished speaking the drop fell, and together the brothers expiated their crime.

RICHARD DAVIES

Another case in which "the one was taken and the other left" was the Crewe murder case, in which Richard and George Davies were found guilty of the murder of their father, with a strong recommendation to mercy on account of their youth. So far as could be made out, there was absolutely no difference in the degrees of their guilt; but the sentence of George was commuted to penal servitude simply because he was the younger. At this there was great excitement throughout the country, and thousands of telegrams and petitions were poured into the Home Office, begging that the leniency might be equally extended to both since the guilt of both was equal. But all to no purpose. The condemned lad protested, to his last moments, that although he took part in the murder, he never struck his father nor handled the hatchet with which the deed was done. He wrote most affectionate letters to his mother, brothers and sisters; who seemed to fully believe the truth of his statements with regard to his share in the crime. Ten minutes before his death he wrote out the same declaration and handed it to the chaplain. He stated that he had no wish to live, but that he hoped and expected to meet his relations in heaven. When I entered his cell he was pale, but calm. After pinioning him his face seemed still paler and his mouth worked convulsively as he strove to keep back his emotion. Along the corridor he walked firmly, with bent head, but when we reached the yard where a fresh breeze was blowing and the blue sky was visible, he raised his head and eyes for a last look at the world and the sky. He died firmly, with a brief prayer on his lips.

* * * * *

In both the cases last described the action of the Home Secretary was very severely commented upon by press and public, and it seems to me that such occurrences are the strongest possible arguments in favour of the re-arrangement of the law which I suggest in the chapter on "Capital Punishment." It is decidedly injurious for the public to have the idea that the life or death of a man depends upon the urgency of the petitions in his favour and the amount of sympathy expressed for him, rather than upon the justice of the case. Moreover, it seems to me that by singling out special cases, and attacking the decision of the Home Office, the press and the public place themselves in a thoroughly illogical position. If they object to the system of leaving the matter in the hands of the Home Secretary, surely it is the system, and not the man, that should be attacked. On the other hand, if they are satisfied that the Home Secretary is the proper tribunal, they ought surely to rest content with his ruling, remembering that he has far better opportunities of judging the merits of the case and the whole of the evidence than any outsider can possibly have, and that his responsibility in the matter makes him more careful in his enquiry than any outsider possibly can be.

* * * * *

The melancholy interest of the subject allures me to continue, yet the details of murderers' deaths at the best are ghastly and grim, and I fear that my readers will shudderingly wish me to stop. Two more experiences, and I will close the sad record.

MARY ELEANOR WHEELER

Better known as Mrs. Pearcey, was a woman of decidedly strong character. Her crime is so recent and aroused so much interest that I need not go over the circumstances. The night before her execution was spent in the condemned cell, watched by three female warders, who stated that her fortitude was remarkable. When introduced to her I said, "Good morning, Madam," and she shook my proffered hand without any trace of emotion. She was certainly the most composed person in the whole party. Sir James Whitehead, the Sheriff of the County of London, asked her if she wished to make any statement, as her last opportunity for doing so was fast approaching, and after a moment's pause she said:—"My sentence is a just one, but a good deal of the evidence against me was false." As the procession was formed and one of the female warders stepped to each side of the prisoner, she turned to them with a considerate desire to save them the pain of the death scene, and said, "You have no need to assist me, I can walk by myself." One of the women said that she did not mind, but was ready and willing to accompany Mrs. Pearcey, who answered, "Oh, well, if you don't mind going with me, I am pleased." She then kissed them all and quietly proceeded to her painless death.

Mrs. Pearcey

JOHN CONWAY

Who murdered a boy of ten years old, at Liverpool, was a case that was most difficult to understand. His previous record did not indicate any quarrelsome or murderous tendency, though he was known to get drunk occasionally; and there seemed to be absolutely no motive that could be assigned for the crime. His confession was made privately, to the priest, the day before his execution, with instructions that it should be read as soon as he was dead, but it left the matter of motive as mysterious as ever. It was as follows:—"In confessing my guilt I protest that my motive was not outrage. Such a thought I never in all my life entertained. Drink has been my ruin, not lust. I was impelled to the crime while under the influence of drink, by a fit of murderous mania, and a morbid curiosity to observe the process of dying. A moment after the commission of the crime I experienced the deepest sorrow of it, and would have done anything in the world to undo it." Conway was a very superstitious man, a believer in omens, witchcraft and all sorts of supernatural powers, and he had a firm idea that if one good man could be induced to pray for him he would be saved from execution. He was sure that his own prayers would avail nothing, and he thought that he was not fit to receive the sacrament of his church; but he attended the service at which the sacrament was administered, and begged that one of his fellow-prisoners, who partook of the rite, should pray for him. As he reached the scaffold Conway stared wildly around and cried out that he wanted to say something. The priest interfered to induce me to stop the execution for a few seconds, and I did so, but the convict merely thanked the gaol officials and his Father Confessor for their kindness. And so he died.

John Conway

Does the reader think that I have spun out this chapter too much? Does he think that I have unnecessarily harrowed his feelings? If so, let me assure him that I would not have given this chapter, I would not have written this book if I had not had what I believe to be good purposes in view. I have tried to avoid sensationalism, but I want to make every reader *think*. I want to make him think that murderers are, after all, men and women, with human sympathies and passions. I want to make him think that there are degrees of murder, that justice, and not spasmodic leniency should be the aim of our laws, and a few other thoughts that will occur to the reader without any suggestion of mine.

Lancaster Castle

CHAPTER IX

FROM THE MURDERER'S POINT OF VIEW

BURNS sang, and we are fond of repeating his singing:—

Oh! wad some power the giftie gie us,
To see oursels as ithers see us;

but I never heard anybody utter the opposite aspiration, for the gift to see others as they see themselves. And yet I am not quite sure that this gift is not as desirable as the other. At any rate, if we are to legislate wisely and well for any class of people it is absolutely necessary that we should be able to see things from their own point of view. It is with much hesitation that I start this chapter, for I know that my power to analyze thought and character is not great enough to enable me to deal with the subject on broad lines. But if I can induce a few people to consider the question of murder and its punishment from the murderer's point of view, the chapter will do good.

On the whole, I think that our attitude towards murderers is based too much on sentiment and too little on reason. Many people pity all murderers, whether they deserve it or not; many others condemn them body, soul and spirit, without considering to what extent they are the result of circumstances. If I can induce my readers to consider that a murderer has as much right to judge the State as the State has to judge him, I think this book will have achieved one good purpose.

I do not wish to work out an argument, but will just give a few of the expressed ideas of the murderers, in the hope that they may give rise to fruitful trains of thought. I would point out, however, that many of the people who have died on the scaffold have lived in such deplorable circumstances—assailed by every sort of temptation, surrounded by an atmosphere of gay and hollow vice, cradled in misery and educated in wretchedness and sin, with little of the good and the beautiful entering into their lives to raise them, but with the accursed facility for obtaining drink to lure them down—in such deplorable circumstances, I say, that even an angel could hardly keep himself unspotted from such a world. When men commit a horrible crime it is our duty to exact the penalty; but it will do us no harm to consider whether we are in any way responsible for the conditions which may have driven them to crime; and whether we cannot do even more than we are doing for the prevention of crime by the improvement of the conditions.

Besides the conditions of life, the mental status of the wretched culprits should be worthy of attention, and I think we might ask ourselves whether it would not have been better for some of the murderers, as well as for society, if they had been placed under life-long restraint years before their careers reached the murder stage.

There are many other questions which will naturally occur to the thoughtful reader, and which I need not indicate.

ARTHUR SHAW

Amongst my earlier executions was that of Arthur Shaw at Liverpool. Shaw was a tailor, thirty-one years of age, who lived in Manchester. He was married, but his married life was not happy, for his wife seems to have drunk heavily, and he himself was not steady. On November 3rd, 1884, they quarrelled, and fought for some time, and shortly afterwards the woman was found dead— killed, according to the doctors, by strangulation. Shaw did not deny the murder, but pleaded that it was unintentional, and that he had been greatly provoked by his wife's long-continued dissipation. The jury strongly recommended him to mercy. Immediately before meeting his fate, in a last conversation with the chaplain, the man admitted his guilt but earnestly insisted that he had never intended to cause his wife's death. He stated that he was not drunk at the time of the murder, but that he had been driven to drink by his wife's drunkenness and neglect of the home, which was always miserable; and that her drunkenness and neglect exasperated him until he was perfectly wild. He concluded by saying: "When we were having the scuffle I had no idea I was killing the poor woman."

THOMAS PARRY

hanged in Galway on January 20th, 1885, for the murder of Miss Burns, wrote a long statement, which he handed to the governor to be read after his death. The gist of it was given in the following paragraph:—"I wish to assure the public and my family and friends that I was of unsound mind for a week previous to the murder and for some time afterwards. I am happy to suffer for the crime which I committed, and confident that I shall enter upon an eternity of bliss. I die at peace with all men, and hope that anyone that I have ever injured will forgive me."

GEORGE HORTON,

of Swanwick, poisoned his little daughter; for the purpose, it is supposed, of obtaining the sum of £7 for which her life was insured; and was executed at Derby on February 1st, 1886. It is difficult, or impossible, for an ordinary person to understand such a man's frame of mind. One would think him absolutely callous, yet he wept over the body of his child when he found that she was dead, and wrote most affectionate letters to his other children when he was in prison. A portion of his last letter to his eldest daughter was as follows:—

You must be sure to pray to God to gide you all you life through and you must pray for your Brothers and Sisters i do pray to God to gard you all you life through. So my dear Daughter you must think of what i have told you. you must always tell the truth & when you are tempted to do wrong you must pray to God for his help and he will hear you. Always remember that my Dear Children, and you must tell the others the same, you that is your brothers and sisters God has promised to be a father to you all ways, remember that he sees all you do and all you think, then if you do his will while here on earth he will receive you to his throne in glory where all is peace and rest. So my Dear Children you will be able to meat all your brothers and sisters and your poore dear Mother in heaven, and by the help of God i shall meat you there to . . . may God help you all and bless you and keep you all your lifes through. He will do it if you pray to him and ask him. You no you must take every think to God in prayer for you no you will have no one els to help you now. so no more from your loving father, George Horton. May God bless you all. Kisses for you all.

Edward Pritchard

EDWARD PRITCHARD

was an instance of how "evil communications corrupt good manners," and a striking example of the unfortunate uselessness of our reformatory system. At twelve years of age he was convicted for being an "associate of thieves," and sentenced to two years in a reformatory. For three years after leaving the reformatory he managed to keep out of prison, but when seventeen he was sentenced to four months' imprisonment for shop-breaking, and after this he was frequently in gaol. About a year before the murder he appeared to have reformed, attended Sunday-school and chapel, and took an active part in religious work right up to the time of committing the murder. He murdered a small boy of fourteen who was in the habit of regularly fetching money from the bank to pay the wages at a

103

large factory, and stole from him the wages money, amounting to over £200. The evidence of the deed was absolutely conclusive and overwhelming, and Pritchard had no hope of reprieve. A day or two after his conviction he wrote a letter to one of his Sunday-school teachers, in which he professed to have seen the error of his ways, urged all his companions to shun bad company, drinking and smoking, spoke of the delight with which he remembered some of the Sunday-school hymns, and anticipated the pleasure of soon singing them "up there." All through his life there seems to have been a struggle between good and evil, with an unfortunate balance of power on the side of evil. It is difficult to believe that he would have devoted his spare time for a year to religious work if he had not felt strong aspirations for the higher life. After conviction he said but little about himself, and made no formal statement or confession, but a letter which he wrote to the father of the murdered boy will throw some light upon his mental state. In this letter Pritchard distinctly affirms that he was led to commit the crime by the instigation of a companion, and though the statements of a convicted murderer must always be received with caution, it is possible that there was some ground for this assertion. If the crime was really suggested and the criminal encouraged by the influence of another, and probably a stronger mind, we may well ask ourselves how much of the moral blame attaches to the instigator, and how much to the weak tool. The letter was as follows:—

Her Majesty's Prison,
Monday, Feb. 14th.

Sir,

I write these lines to you to express my deep sorrow for the dreadful crime I have done to you and to your master. I write to ask you if you and your wife will forgive me for killing your boy, and please ask the master if he will forgive me for taking his

104

money from him. It would not have happened if I had not been incited to do it, and it was by no other person than —— ——, who was a witness against me. He persuaded me to do it, and said he might do it himself if I did not; so I done the unhappy affair. I am very sorry I ever met with —— at all, but it cannot be called back now. I have cried to God for mercy; I must still cry, and I hope I shall gain a better home. I have asked Him to forgive me and blot out all my sins, and wash me in my Saviour's precious blood; and I think and feel He will do it. I'm going to receive the Holy Communion on Wednesday, and I should like to hear from you by Wednesday, before I go to be partaker of that holy feast. If you will forgive me, I shall be more at peace.

I am very, very sorry indeed, for what I have done. There is nothing that can save me from my doom, which will be on Thursday, but I can ask God to have mercy on my poor soul.

I have no more to say at present, only that I was a great friend of poor Harry, and I went nearly mad about it the first few nights, and could not sleep; but now I find comfort in Jesus. Good-bye, Sir. Please send me an answer by return of post, and I hope we shall meet in Heaven.

From EDWARD PRITCHARD.

Gloucester County Gaol,
Gloucestershire.

A few particulars of Pritchard's last moments are given in "How Murderers Die"

Alfred Scandrett

ALFRED SCANDRETT,

another young man—only just twenty-one years old—was another example of the result of bad influences. His father deserted the home when Alfred was about ten years old. His mother was a hard-working woman who contrived to support her family by mangling and by selling papers in the streets, in which latter work she was assisted by Alfred and several other children. The lad was fond of hanging round street corners and public-houses, and his mother found it impossible to keep him at home like the other children. He continually made resolutions, but again and again he was led away by his companions, and at twelve years of age he was convicted for stealing cigars from a shop, but discharged with a caution. A month later he was charged with another offence and sentenced to 21 days. Other imprisonments followed, then five years in a reformatory, but punishment was no cure. His love for his mother was his one redeeming feature, and if she had not been forced by grinding

106

poverty to work almost day and night at her mangling and paper-hawking she might have succeeded in saving him from himself. He tried to break away from his evil associations, and at one time begged his mother to find money to take him to Canada, but she was utterly unable to scrape together enough to pay the passage. A youth called Jones, who was hanged with Scandrett, was his companion in his final crime—a burglary, ending in murder. Although attached to his mother, who said he had always been "a good lad" to her, Scandrett could not bear the idea of living at home when he was engaged in crime, so that almost the whole of the last eight years of his life was spent, when out of gaol, in common lodging-houses. After his conviction for murder and sentence to death, his great anxiety was for his mother. And well might he be anxious, for the poor woman suffered sadly for his sin. As soon as it was known that she was "the mother of a murderer," her customers—to their eternal disgrace be it said—withdrew their patronage to such an extent that her mangling earnings dropped from 12s. or 14s. to 2s. a week, and her newspaper trade fell away to nothing. She was even "hunted" and insulted in the streets when she went to her accustomed corner to sell the papers. To get from her home in Birmingham to Hereford Gaol for a last interview with her son, she was obliged to pawn her dress, and even that only raised enough money to pay the fare one way, so that she had to trust to chance for the means of getting back again. Some of the prison officials, more humane than her "friends" at home, subscribed enough money to pay the return fare. The last meeting was a very affecting one. Scandrett comforted his mother by assuring her that they would meet in heaven, and said, "Pray daily and hourly, mother, as I have done, and then we shall meet in heaven."

ARTHUR DELANEY

The number of men who are driven to crime through drink is something terrible, and I should think that no temperance worker could read the real histories of the murderers who have come under my hands without redoubling his efforts to save men from the curse of drink. A case in point was Arthur Delaney, executed at Chesterfield on August 10th, 1888. It may be said that he was naturally a bad, violent man, but surely he would never have become a murderer if he had not consistently made himself worse and worse by hard drinking. His victim was his wife, to whom he had been married four years, and who was spoken of as a respectable, hard-working woman. Not very long after the marriage, in a drunken fit, he violently assaulted her, for which action the magistrates imposed a fine and granted a separation order. His wife, however, forgave him, and in spite of his bad behaviour continued to live with him. A few days before the murder he was unusually violent, and treated his wife so brutally that she was obliged to again appeal to the magistrates, who again imposed a fine. This raised Delaney's anger to such an extent that the next time he got drunk he battered his wife so violently that she had to be removed to the hospital, where she died. Like many other culprits, Delaney saw the cause of the mischief when it was done; and a letter written after his sentence, has a ring of simple earnestness about it that makes it worth preserving. It was written to some Good Templars who had tried to reform him.

H.M. Prison, Derby,
August 8th, 1888.

My Dear Friends,

I write you farewell on this earth, but hope with gods great mercy to meet you all there, were there will be no more sorrow or temptation. I do sincerely thank you for your kindness to me, and hope that my fall will be the means of, with god's help of lifting others up from a drunkard's grave. Had I followed your advise my poor wife would been alive now, and we should have been happy, for she was a faithful and good wife to me. God knows that I should not have done such a dreadful crime if I had kept my pledge, but hope it will be a warning to those that play with the devil in solution. Will you tell —— to give his heart to god, and he will be safe from his great curse, the drink. Bid him and his wife farewell for me, and tell him to put all his powers to work to help the Noble work of Temperance onward, for it is God's work. Oh! do implore them that is playing with the drink to abstain from it, for it is a national curse. Now farewell to you all, and may God prosper your noble work.

From your unfortunate friend,

ARTHUR T. DELANEY.

What proportion of murders is directly traceable to drink it would be very difficult to say, but time after time we find that murderers who write to their friends state that drink, and drink only, has caused their ruin.

ELIZABETH BERRY

Although I am endeavouring in this chapter to give a few ideas of the motives for murder as seen by the murderers themselves, I am not by any means condoning their crimes. My main object is to induce people to look more into the pre-disposing causes of crime. I want them to consider whether in many cases prevention is not better than cure, and whether more can not be done to remove the causes. Undoubtedly drink has to answer for the largest number of such crimes. After drink comes lust and jealousy, though these almost invariably reach the murder climax through drink. The other main motive is the love of money, which has led to many of the most heartless, inhuman deeds that it has been my lot to avenge. I have given one or two instances of parents who murdered their own children for the sake of a few pounds of insurance money, and such instances could be multiplied. In fact, so apparent did the motive become a year or two back, that the Government was obliged to pass a law regulating the insurance of the lives of infants. If such an act, or even a further-reaching one, had been in existence earlier, Elizabeth Berry might have been alive now instead of lying in a felon's grave. Mrs. Berry poisoned her daughter, aged 11. At the time of the murder the child's life was insured for £10, for which Mrs. Berry was paying a premium of 1d. per week. The murderess had also made a proposal for a mutual insurance on her own life and the child's by which £100 should be paid, on the death of either, to the survivor. She was under the impression that the policy was completed, but as a matter of fact, it was not. It seems almost impossible that a woman should murder a child for the sake of gaining even the full sum of £110; and we might be justified in believing that there must be some other motive if it were not for the fact that infanticide has been committed again and again for much smaller sums. From the point of view of the murderers of children it would seem that a few pounds in money appears a sufficient inducement to soil their hands with the blood of a fellow-creature. It is well, therefore, for the sake of child-life that the temptation should be removed.

Mrs. Berry

CHAPTER X

ON CAPITAL PUNISHMENT

ONE of the questions which is most frequently put to me is, whether I consider capital punishment is a right and proper thing. To this I can truly answer that I do. For my own part I attach much weight to the Scripture injunction, "Whoso sheddeth man's blood, by man shall his blood be shed," and I think that the abolition of capital punishment would be a defiance of the divine command. Therefore I would not abolish capital punishment altogether, but, as I shall explain later, I would greatly alter the conditions under which it is imposed.

Perhaps many of my readers will say that the Scriptural command should have no weight, and others will say that it was a command given under the "dispensation of Law," while we live under the "dispensation of Grace." Therefore I would argue that, quite apart from any consideration of a religious nature, capital punishment is absolutely necessary for the checking of the greatest criminals.

In the discharge of my duties as a policeman, both in the Nottingham, in the Bradford, and in the West Riding Police force, I have had many chances of studying the ways of life and thought of the criminal classes, and I have paid a great deal of attention to the subject. As the result of my experience I can safely say that capital punishment, and "the cat," are the only legal penalties that possess any real terrors for the hardened criminal, for the man who might be called a "professional" as distinguished from an "amateur" ruffian. Such a man does what he can to keep out of prison, because he dislikes restraint, and routine, and sobriety, but this dislike is not strong enough to deter him from any crime which offers even a chance of escaping scot-free; and I do not think that the fear of imprisonment ever occurs to him when he has once got criminal work actually in hand. Penal servitude, even for life, has no very acute terrifying influence, partly because no criminal ever believes that it will be a reality in his case, as he feels sure that he will get a commutation of sentence; and partly because, even if he were sure that the imprisonment were actually for life, he knows that prison life is not such a dreadful fate, after all—when one gets used to it. But when it comes to a question of a death sentence it is quite another matter. Death is a horrible mystery, and a death on the scaffold, a cold-blooded, pre-determined, and ignominious death is especially horrible to the criminal mind. As a rule the most desperate criminals are those who are most terrified by the thought of death at the hands of the executioner, possibly, because the most desperate men spring from the most superstitious class of the community, and have the greatest dread of that "something" after death which they cannot define.

The criminal classes do not neglect their newspapers, but keep themselves pretty well posted, either by reading or conversation, upon the subjects that are of most direct interest to them, and follow all the details of the most important criminal trials. In this way they always keep more or less before them the thought of the nature of capital punishment, and I believe that it will be found that the number of capital crimes in any given period is inversely proportionate to the number of capital punishments in the immediately preceding period. Whenever there is a series of executions, without reprieves, the number of murders decreases, and on the other hand, after a period in which several persons have been tried for murder and acquitted, or reprieved after sentence, the number of crimes appears to increase. I do not think that this rule can be demonstrated forcibly and convincingly by a reference to the mere numbers of murders, convictions, reprieves, and executions during the past few years, because there are many considerations which bear upon the significance of an execution or reprieve; but I think that anyone who has given attention to the subject will bear me out in my contention.

Undoubtedly the fear of death is a great deterring power amongst abandoned men, and the fear is most powerful when the death seems most certain and the hope of reprieve most remote. This consideration leads me to think that the deterrent value of the death sentence would be greatly increased if it could be made absolutely irrevocable. Considering capital punishment as a moral power for frightening criminals still at large, I think it would be much better, if in all cases where there is the slightest possible chance of reprieve, the sentence were suspended for a time.

I advocate that the sentence of death, once passed, should be a sentence which the doomed man, as well as his friends and sympathisers who are still at liberty, should regard as quite irrevocable. At the same time I do not advocate an increase in the number of executions—just the reverse. As the best means to this end I think we ought to have a considerable alteration in our criminal law as it relates to murder cases. I think that the jury should have more power over the sentence, and for this purpose I think that they ought to have the choice of five classes of verdict, namely:—

1. Not guilty.
2. Not proven.
3. Murder in the third degree.
4. Murder in the second degree.
5. Murder in the first degree.

In the case of a verdict of "Not Guilty" the prisoner would, of course, be acquitted, and would be a free man as he is with such a verdict at present.

In the case of the verdict of "Not Proven" it should be within

114

the power of the judge to remand the prisoner, pending the further investigation of any clues that might seem likely to throw light upon the case; or to release him, either with or without bail or police supervision.

A verdict of "Murder in the third degree" would be brought in in cases where there was undoubted proof of the crime being committed by the prisoner, but in which the circumstances were such as to make it extremely unlikely that the prisoner would ever again commit a violent crime. This would cover the cases of people who shoot their friends and then plead that they "did not think it was loaded," and would be a much better verdict than the "accidental death" which is generally returned at present. When the jury find this verdict of murder in the third degree it should rest with the judge to impose a term of imprisonment, long or short, according to the circumstances.

"Murder in the second degree" would embrace cases in which the murder was fully proved but in which there was not premeditation or intent to murder. Under this head would come a number of deaths resulting from rows, brawls, and assaults without intent to kill. The judge would have the power to pass a sentence of death or of penal servitude for life.

"Murder in the first degree," in which both intent and result had been murder, would be a verdict leaving the judge no option but to impose the death penalty.

Another question which ought to be considered in this connection is the question of appeals. At present appeals are made to the Home Secretary. He is really assisted by a number of other gentlemen, who examine most thoroughly into the original evidence, and any additional evidence that may have turned up, but this is a tribunal not legally appointed, and the public notion is that in cases of appeal the reversal of the sentence lies in the hands of one man. I do not think that even the most abandoned wretches would impute any unfairness to the English Home Secretary, but I know that in many quarters there is an idea that the Home Secretary is "a very kind gentleman," who will "let 'em off" if he possibly can, and such an idea seems to be a very mischievous one. A court of appeal would appear less personal, and would be far less likely to be suspected of leniency if it consisted of three judges, one of whom should be the judge who had originally tried the case. To such a bench of judges I would allow appeals to be made, and would give them power to re-open cases, refer them back to the juries, or to modify sentences, but not to reverse a jury's verdict. This would mean that in the case of a verdict of "murder in the first degree," the only way in which the execution could be prevented would be by referring the case back to the jury, and this should only be done on the production of new evidence pointing to a miscarriage of justice. In the extreme case of evidence turning up at the last moment, the Home Secretary should have power to grant a stay of execution for such length of time as would allow the bench of judges to re-open the case.

The drawing up and presentation of petitions by people who are in no way connected with the case, would to a great extent be done away with under such a system as I have outlined, but in order to provide for cases where the system might not have this effect, I would make it a punishable offence to attempt to influence the decision of the judges or jurymen, by an appeal to any consideration other than the evidence. This advice I give because in so many, nay, in most cases, the appeals contained in petitions are based upon considerations other than the justice of the case. If the condemned person is an interesting character, or if there is any sort of excuse upon which an appeal can be based, there are always a great number of people who have no special knowledge of the case, and who, perhaps, have not even read the newspaper reports, who are ready to get up petitions, collect signatures, and stir up a lot of sympathy for one who too often deserves nothing but execration and contempt. Such agitations lead to much misrepresentation of facts, and often to sweeping condemnations of the judge and jury. They tend to infuse, in the minds of young people especially, an incorrect notion that the administration of the law is uncertain and ineffectual, even if it is not unjust and corrupt.

The mere fact of the extent to which the consideration of loathsome crimes and their punishment is brought under the notice of children by this system of petitions, is in my mind sufficient argument for its complete suppression. One case I might instance, in which the masters of two public schools led the whole of the children under their charge through an ante-room in which a petition was lying, and made them all sign it in turn. This kind of thing occurs whenever a petition praying for a sentence of death to be reversed or commuted is in the course of signature, and surely such a thing should not be possible.

In many cases the people who draw up these petitions are people who object on principle to all capital punishment, but unfortunately the principle is entirely lost to sight when dealing with individual cases. The fact of big petitions being presented in one case, while no effort is made in another case with similar features, naturally leads uneducated people to think that there is uncertainty and injustice about the whole affair.

There is still one other respect in which I think that our law with reference to murder and the death penalty ought to be altered, and that is with regard to the length of time allowed to elapse between sentence and execution. In the interests of all concerned I would reduce the time from three clear weeks, as at present, to one week only. No doubt many readers will cry out against this as an unnecessary cruelty to the condemned, but I say that I would do it in the interests of *all* after full consideration and an unusually full knowledge of the ideas of the condemned upon the subject. It is not a shorter time that would be a cruelty—the present long time is where the real cruelty comes in.

So far as I know, the three weeks' "grace" given to the condemned man is intended as a time for repentance and for attending to the affairs of the soul. Therefore, the question of allowing a long or short time is to a great extent a religious one, and dangerous for me to tackle, so I will confine my remarks as far as possible to matters of fact and mere common-sense considerations. If the only purpose of the time allowed between sentence and execution is to admit of conversion and a preparation for heaven, it is fair to ask of anyone who wishes to continue the present system, whether it serves the purpose. If not, there would seem to be no valid argument in favour of its continuance. Personally, I am convinced by long experience, that the hope of regeneration during three weeks in the case of murderers is absolutely vain. There are many instances in which the criminal becomes "penitent," as it is sometimes termed, and these penitents may be divided into two classes. Firstly, there is the class of those who have committed murder without intent or premeditation. In a fit of frenzy or under peculiar circumstances they have killed a human being. It may be a half-starved mother who has killed the baby she could not feed, or a man who in a whirlwind of temper has killed the unfaithful and miserable wife whose conduct has made his life a hell upon earth for years. It may be many another similar case which under the scheme of five possible verdicts, propounded above, would be returned as murder in the second or third degree. Under such a law the extreme penalty would not be imposed; but while we are under our present law, and supposing that these persons are condemned, without chance of reprieve, we may fairly ask whether the three weeks' grace is an advantage to them. Such criminals are truly repentant, or rather, remorseful. As a rule, the enormity of the crime bursts upon them in the first calm moment after its commission. They recoil in horror from the deed they have done and would gladly sacrifice anything, even life itself, to undo that deed again. There is true repentance, which I take it is the key to forgiveness, even before their apprehension and condemnation. Everything that can be done on earth by or for such poor souls, can be done in a week, and they would not ask for more. Their repentance is sincere, their horror of their crime is greater than their dread of death, which they welcome as a means of expiation. Is any good purpose served by keeping such people for three weeks in agony?

The second class of "penitents" consists of a horrible section of humanity—the cowardly desperadoes. These are usually men whose crimes have shown a refinement of cruelty and callousness that is positively revolting. They are the "hardened" or professional criminals whose hearts are devoid of pity or remorse, and equally devoid of the least spark of courage. They are the miserable men whose lives have been spent in defying and blaspheming God, but who, when they see death before them, whine and howl, and beg for the intercession of the chaplain or any other godly person they may meet with, not because they repent of their sins, but because they are frightened almost to death by the thought of a fiery hell, which has been painted before their imaginations in glowing colours. To such men as these I am sure that the shortening of the waiting time would be the greatest possible mercy, for the longer time only gives them opportunity to work themselves into an almost demented state. At the end of three weeks they are often so broken down and hysterical as to be incapable of correctly understanding anything, and their only remaining feeling is a wild, frantic dread of the scaffold.

Besides the two classes of penitents, there only remains the class who are not penitent at all. They are mostly men who have been long acquainted with crime, who have made it the business of their lives. They look upon the law and its officers much as a business man looks upon a clever and unscrupulous competitor; and upon a sentence of death as one of the business risks. Life ends for them, not at the scaffold, but in the dock, when sentence is pronounced. From that time they sink into a state of sullen indifference, or take up any occupation that may offer, merely to kill time. In some cases they take to Bible reading and prayers, because they think "it can't do any harm, and may do a bit of good," and because they have nothing else to do. No one can say that such men are penitent, since on release they would return

119

to their vicious ways. They would not be likely to reach any better state if they were allowed to live three months instead of three weeks, for the only regret that they can be brought to feel is personal and purely selfish. It is founded on fear of hell, and is not a contrition for having committed the crime, but a regret that the crime carries with it a punishment in the next world. Convicts of this class, when they have no hope of reprieve, do not thank us for the three weeks of "life" that are given to them. If they could have their own choice, they would prefer to walk straight from the dock to the scaffold, and to "get it over" at once.

In every case if the matter is thoroughly inquired into, on lines of common sense instead of mere sentiment, I think the conclusion will be that the three weeks allowed are no advantage whatever to the convicts. In most cases their position would be decidedly improved by reducing the time.

There are other distinct advantages to be gained by reducing the interval. In the first place it would greatly improve the moral effect of the death sentence. Retribution following directly after conviction is a distinct object lesson, and the shorter the time between, the more obvious is the connection between the crime and the punishment. When even three weeks elapse the connection is often lost.

In the second place, the alteration I advocate would greatly prevent the stirring up of false sentiment in favour of convicts who happen to have an interesting personality. It would put a stop to the petition signing which is often indulged in by people who know nothing of the case, but who are worked upon to express sympathy with the convict, and want of faith in the justice of our system of trial. If only a week elapsed between sentence and execution, the facts of the trial and details of the evidence would remain fresher in the public mind, and people would be less liable to be led to mistrust the justice of the sentence.

To all the people who have charge of the convicts before execution, a shortening of the time would be a great blessing, for such a charge is often a soul-harrowing experience. The chaplains especially, whose experiences are often most unpleasant; and whose earnest efforts meet with such disappointing return, would, I think, welcome the change.

Norwich Castle

CHAPTER XI

HANGING: FROM A BUSINESS POINT OF VIEW

I HAVE stated in Chapter II. the reasons which led me to take the office of executioner. The reader will remember that I then claimed no higher motive than a desire to obtain a living for my family, by an honest trade. I am not ashamed of my calling, because I consider that if it is right for men to be executed (which I believe it is, in murder cases) it is right that the office of executioner should be held respectable. Therefore, I look at hanging from a business point of view.

When I first took up the work I was in the habit of applying to the Sheriff of the County whenever a murderer was condemned to death. I no longer consider it necessary to apply for work in England, because I am now well known, but I still send a simple address card, as above, when an execution in Ireland is announced.

In the earlier days I made application on a regular printed form, which gave the terms and left no opening for mistake or misunderstanding. Of this form I give a reduced reproduction on opposite page. I still use this circular when a sheriff from whom I have had no previous commission writes for terms. The travelling expenses are understood to include second-class railway fare from Bradford to the place of execution and back, and cab fare from railway station to gaol. If I am not lodged in the gaol, hotel expenses are also allowed. As a rule the expenses are not closely reckoned, but the sheriffs vote a lump sum which they think will cover it; and if the execution has been satisfactory the sum granted is generally more than enough to cover what I have spent.

There are, on an average, some twenty executions annually, so that the reader can calculate pretty nearly what is my remuneration for a work which carries with it a great deal of popular odium, which is in many ways disagreeable, and which may be accompanied, as it has been in my own experience, by serious danger, resulting in permanent bodily injury. It will be seen that the net commission is not by any means an exorbitant annual sum, considering all the circumstances of the office; and that it does not approach the amount which some people have stated that I was able to earn.

Of course, my earnings are entirely uncertain, since they wholly depend upon the number of executions, and this arrangement, by which my livelihood depends upon the number of poor fellows condemned to die, is, to me, the most repugnant feature of my work. It seems a horrible thing that I should have to peruse newspaper reports in the hope that a fellow-creature may be condemned to death, whenever I wish to feel sure that "business is not falling off;" and that I should have to regard as evil days and hard times those periods when there seem to be lulls in the annals of crime, and when one might reasonably hope that a better state of things was dawning in the land.

QUOTE
No.

Bradford,_____189

YORKS.

Sir,

I beg leave to state in reply to your letter

of the _____ that I

am prepared to undertake the execution you name of

_____

at _____ on the _____

I also beg leave to state that my terms are as

follows: £10 for the execution, £5 if the condemned

is reprieved, together with all travelling expenses.

Awaiting your reply,

I am, Sir,

Your obedient Servant,

James Berry.

The High Sheriff,

for the County of _____

These considerations, and the more selfish but still perfectly natural wish to be certain of my income and of my ability to give my children a fair start in life, have led me to strongly approve of the suggestion that the executioner's office should be a Government appointment, with a fixed salary instead of an uncertain commission. When the Lords' Committee on Capital Punishment was sitting, early in 1887, I expressed my views on this matter in a letter addressed to the President of the Committee, Lord Aberdare. I am not without hope that a change in the arrangements for regulating the office of executioner will ere long be made, and the lines on which I think that it might be most reasonably and satisfactorily done, are set forth in the letter to Lord Aberdare, which I append.

1, *Bilton Place,*
City Road, Bradford.
February, 1887.

My LORD,

I have been for some time past in correspondence with Mr. Howard Vincent, M.P. for Sheffield, with reference to alteration in the mode of remunerating my services, in carrying into effect the Sentence of the Law upon Criminals convicted of Capital Crimes. Mr. Howard Vincent has suggested that I should address myself to the Honourable Committee on Capital Punishment, through your Lordship as their President.

I would therefore respectfully point out to your Lordship and your Honourable Committee that the present mode of payment for my services is unsatisfactory and undesirable, and that a change is needed.

As your Lordship is doubtless aware, under the existing arrangements I am paid the sum of £10 together with travelling and other incidental expenses for each Execution conducted by me. There are, on an average, roughly speaking, 25 Executions yearly. What I would respectfully suggest is, that, instead of this payment by Commission, I should receive a fixed salary from the Government of £350 per annum. I may say that since accepting the Appointment I have never received less than £270 in any one year. I am informed that in determining a fixed Salary, or Compensation in lieu of a payment by Commission, the average annual amount received is made the basis for the calculation.

It will be apparent to your Lordship that an offer of a *less* sum than the former average would not be sufficiently advantageous to induce me to exchange the old system for the new. I may further, with your Lordship's permission, draw attention to the peculiar Social position in which I am placed by reason of holding the office before referred to. I am to a great extent alone in the world, as a certain social ostracism is attendant upon such office, and extends, not to myself alone, but also includes the members of my family. It therefore becomes extremely desirable that my children should, for their own sakes, be sent to a school away from this town. To do this of course would entail serious expenditure, only to be incurred in the event of my being able to rely on a fixed source of income, less liable to variation than the present remuneration by Commission alone. I am also unable for obvious reasons to obtain any other employment. My situation as boot salesman held by me previous to my acceptance of the Office of Executioner, had to be given up on that account alone, my employer having no fault to find with me, but giving that as the sole reason for dispensing with my services.

My late Employer will give me a good reference as to General character, and the Governors of Gaols in which I have conducted Executions will be ready to speak as to my steadiness and also my ability and skill on performing the duties devolving upon me.

In conclusion I should be ready to give and call Evidence on the points hereinbefore referred to (if it should seem fit to your Lordship and your Honourable Committee), on receiving a notification to that effect.

Under these circumstances I trust that your Lordship will

be able to see the way clear to embody in your Honourable Committee's report a recommendation to the effect that a fixed annual sum of £350 should be paid me for my services rendered in the Office of Executioner.

I have the honour to be
Your Lordship's Obedient humble servant,

JAMES BERRY.

To the Right Honourable LORD ABERDARE.
President, Capital Punishment Committee,
Whitehall, London, S.W.

P.S. If your Honourable Committee has an alternative to the foregoing proposal I would respectfully suggest that I am permanently retained by the Home Office at a nominal sum of £100 a year, exclusive of fees at present paid to me by Sheriffs of different Counties and the usual Expenses.

In connection with this subject I should like to point out that in asking for the office of executioner to be made a recognised and permanent appointment, I am not suggesting any new thing, but merely a return to the conditions in force not much more than fifteen years ago. Up to 1874 the executioner was a permanently established and recognised official. Mr. Calcraft, the last who occupied this position, was retained by the Sheriffs of the City of London, with a fee of £1 1s. 0d. per week, and also had a retainer from Horsemonger Lane Gaol. In addition to his fees he had various perquisites, which made these two appointments alone sufficient for his decent maintenance, and he also undertook executions all over the country, for which he was paid at about the same rate as I am at present, but with perquisites in all cases. In 1874 he retired, and the City of London allowed him a pension of twenty-five shillings a week for life.

Mr. Calcraft's successor was Mr. Wm. Marwood, who had no official status. He had a retaining fee of £20 a year from the Sheriffs of the City of London, but beyond that he had to depend upon the fees for individual executions and reprieves. In his time, also, there were considerable perquisites, for instance, the clothing and personal property possessed by the criminal at the time of his execution became the property of the executioner. These relics were often sold for really fancy prices and formed no mean item in the annual takings. But the sale and exhibition of such curiosities were only pandering to a morbid taste on the part of some sections of the public, and it was ordered by the Government—very rightly, from a public point of view, but very unfortunately for the executioner—that personal property left by the criminals should be burned.

In many other countries the post of executioner is permanent. In some cases it is hereditary, as in France, where it has remained in the Deibler family, passing from sire to son, for a great length of time.

Even in British territory at the present time a permanent official hangsman is not entirely unknown, for in Malta the post is a definite appointment, to which a salary of £30 is attached.

In England the Sheriff is the officer appointed to carry out the executions, and though he is allowed to employ a substitute if he can find one, it would fall to him to personally conduct the execution if no substitute could be obtained. In certain cases, in days gone by, there has been very great difficulty in securing anyone who would undertake the unpleasant duty, though I do not remember any recorded instance of the Sheriff being absolutely unable to engage an executioner.

CHAPTER XII

THE PRESS AND THE PUBLIC

I MIGHT almost head this chapter, "My Critics," for both press and public are constantly criticising my doings. The criticism is generally friendly, though often based on incomplete knowledge of the facts. Of the press-men I must say that they usually seem most kindly disposed, and certainly many of them go to great trouble to extract from me a few statements which they can spin out into an "interview." As a rule I dislike these interviews, for I know that my employers very strongly object to any more sensationalism than is absolutely necessary being imported into the accounts of executions. Unfortunately, with many of the papers, sensationalism is the one thing needful, and when I meet with a really energetic reporter attached to such a paper my position is a very difficult one. If I say little or nothing in answer to his questions, he may spin a fearful and wonderful yarn out of his own head, and out of the gossip and rumours which seem to be constantly afloat, started, I imagine, by needy penny-a-liners. On the other hand, if I submit to the interview as the best way of keeping it within bounds, the "touches of colour" which the interviewer generally thinks it necessary to add, are pretty sure to land me in bother and misunderstanding.

In several instances statements which were calculated to seriously injure me professionally have been published; and though I believe they were inserted with no evil intent, I have been obliged to employ my solicitors to secure their contradiction.

The instance which annoyed me, perhaps, more than

any other was the reporting of a supposed interview in the *Essex County Chronicle.* It was said to be from "an occasional contributor." The interviewer in question tackled me in the hotel where the Sheriff pays the execution fee; entering the room immediately after I had been paid, and just as the Sheriff was driving off. He asked me two or three questions about private matters, which I answered truthfully and straightforwardly, though I was somewhat annoyed by the man and his manner. The "interview" which appeared quite shocked me. Several of the statements were utterly wrong, but what troubled me most was the following paragraph, which was quite at variance with the actual facts, and with the statements which I had made:—

"And what do your friends think of the profession you have taken up?" I asked.

"It killed my mother and brother," he mournfully replied. "When Marwood died I was appointed in his place, and directly my mother knew of it she was taken ill. My father's solicitor then wrote to the Home Office, informing the authorities of this. The result was that I gave up the position, and Binns got the appointment. My mother died soon afterwards, though, and then, when I saw the way in which Binns was going on, I came to the conclusion that he would not hold the place long, and I again wrote to the Home Office stating that my mother was dead and that there was nothing now to prevent my accommodating them if my assistance should be required. Soon after that I was engaged to hang two men at Edinburgh, and I have carried out nearly all the executions since then. My brother had married a girl with plenty of money, and his pride received a blow on my appointment. That was the cause of his death. He was a Liberal and in favour of abolishing capital punishment, but I am a Conservative through and through. Altogether I have buried my mother, two brothers, and two aunts within the last three years."

This was a false and cruel paragraph, the actual facts with regard to the deaths of my relatives being as follows:—1. My aunts died before I took the office, or thought of doing so. 2.

My mother died from cancer on the liver, from which she had been suffering for a long time before I applied for the post; and she died between the time of my first application and the time of second application, when I was appointed for the double execution at Edinburgh. 3. My brother died of low fever, after I had held the office of executioner for about four years.

I do not wish to deny that my choice of the calling of executioner was a disappointment and annoyance to my family; but to say that it caused, or hastened the death of any one of them is to say that which is not true. If I thought that it had really had any such disastrous effect, I hope I am not such a callous and hardened wretch as to make the matter the subject of discussion with a stranger.

One would almost have thought that such statements as the one extracted above would bear their refutation on their face, and that there would be no need to contradict them; but the matter was seriously taken up by the *Daily News*, which made it the subject of a leader, and other papers all over the country extracted from, or commented upon the matter in the *Daily News*.

Of course, I put the matter into the hands of my solicitors, who took steps to stop the original libel, but they were naturally unable to stop its circulation through the country.

Another affair which caused me much annoyance at the time arose in Hereford, from the greed for interesting and sensational "copy" shown by a member of the staff of the *Hereford Times*. He got up some sensational matter to the effect that after the execution of Hill and Williams I retired to a neighbouring hotel where a smoking concert was in progress, and there held a ghastly levee. The worst of this report was that it was based on some foundation of fact, and that a mere colouration of the report made a reasonable and perfectly innocent entertainment appear as if it was something shameful.

The actual facts were that after the execution I was in company with Alderman Barnet, Mayor of Worcester, and a detective sergeant, both of whom were personal friends of mine. With Alderman Barnet I was invited to a social evening held by some of his friends. It was a perfectly private party, and was decorously conducted in every way. When the *Times* representative appeared, as he was known to the gentlemen present, he was invited to join us, simply as a friend. The report of the party was much talked about at the time, and Sir Edwin Lechmere, M.P. for Hereford, made it the subject of a question in the House of Commons.

From time to time a very great number of incorrect and exaggerated statements have been made in the press with regard to almost every detail of my work, and I suppose that so long as the public have a love for the marvellous, and so long as press-men have treacherous memories or vivid imaginations, it will continue to be so. My enormous income is one of the subjects on which the papers most frequently get astray, and it has often been asserted that my earnings amounted to a thousand a year. I only wish that it might be so, if I could make it from an increase of fee rather than an increase in the number of executions, but the reader has in other places correct statements of what my income really amounts to. I never bear malice against my friends of the press for these little distortions of fact, for I know that they mean no harm, and on the whole they have always used me very well.

With regard to the public, their curiosity to see me is much greater than my desire to satisfy it. I have no wish to be followed about and stared at by a crowd, as if I were a monstrosity, and in many cases I have had to go to some trouble to baulk them. This I can do to a certain extent by travelling by other trains than the one I am expected by. In some cases where there are two or three railways into a town, one of which is the direct line from Bradford, I take the direct line to some local station, and there change into a train of another line or into some train running on some local branch line, and so arrive unobserved. At Newcastle, after the execution of Judge, there was a big and enthusiastic crowd waiting to see me and my assistant depart. There were one or two men in the crowd who knew me by sight, and they knew the train by which we were to travel, so they made a raid on the station, and in spite of the efforts of the railway officials and police to keep the place clear they burst through the barriers with a howl of exultation and filled the platform. The plan by which we evaded them was very simple. We walked over the river to Gateshead, and booked from there to Newcastle. Arriving by train in the midst of the people who were looking for us, we attracted no attention whatever, because the folks who knew me were near the entrance gates, expecting us to come into the station in the ordinary way. As we had our tickets for Bradford with us, we simply crossed the platform to our own train, and in due time steamed southward, leaving the disappointed crowd under the firm impression that we had not entered the station.

The first time that I went to Swansea there was a large crowd of people waiting to see me, but they were disappointed, for I had made a little arrangement which completely upset their calculations. It happened that I travelled from Shrewsbury to Swansea with a gentleman who is well known in the latter town. In the train we entered into conversation, and I found that his carriage was to meet him at the station. I therefore asked him if he could recommend me to a good hotel, and was delighted when he said that he would drive me to one, which was just what I wanted. He did not know who I was, and the little crowd that was watching never imagined that the executioner would be riding in their townsman's carriage. Of course, I did not want to stay at the hotel, because I was to lodge in the gaol, but I thanked my friend for the lift, walked into the hotel for a glass of beer while he was driving away, and then walked up to the prison without anyone suspecting my errand.

Whenever I have been in actual contact with crowds in England, their attitude has been friendly. In Ireland such knots of people as may gather are usually the reverse. In England, if there is any sort of demonstration, it is a cheer; in Ireland it is hooting and groaning. But it is seldom, in England, that I meet with any personal demonstration. The crowds that assemble outside the gaols when executions are in progress, are interesting studies. They hail the hoisting of the black flag with a cheer or a groan, that indicates their opinion of the merits of the case. It is curious to notice how the sympathies of this section of the public lean one way or the other, often without any apparent reason. This thought occurred to me very forcibly at the executions of Israel Lipski and William Hunter, who were hanged within a few months of each other.

Israel Lipski

At Lipski's execution the crowd was the largest I have ever seen, many of the people remained hanging about for hours. The excitement was intense, but there was no sympathy for the prisoner. There were many Jews in the crowd, and wherever they were noticed they were hustled and kicked about, and insulted

135

in every imaginable manner; for the hatred displayed by the mob was extended from Lipski to his race. When the black flag was hoisted it was received with three ringing cheers. Altogether, the crowd showed the utmost detestation of the murderer. And yet his crime was no worse than the majority of murders, and there were many things connected with it, and with the circumstances of the miserable man's life, both before and after, which I should have expected to excite some little sympathy; at any rate, amongst people in a similar station of life.

Hunter's execution was the next but one to Lipski's, and his crime was one which has always seemed to me about the most heartless I ever heard of. Hunter was a striker in a foundry by trade, but a tramp by choice. He left his wife and two children and went on tramp, eventually striking up a sort of partnership with a Scotch woman who had six illegitimate children. One of these, a little girl between three and four years of age, went tramping with them, and of course, the poor wee mite was utterly unfit for the exposure and the many miles of walking which they made her accomplish daily. Hunter and the woman were both cruel to the child, and carried their cruelty to such an extent that on one occasion at any rate, they were remonstrated with, and eventually turned out of a common lodging-house on account of their conduct. At last, one day after a long tramp, the little mite began to cry from weariness, and Hunter, to stop her crying, beat her with a switch. Later, for the same purpose, he thrashed her with a stick that he picked up in the road. Still later in the day he continued his ill-treatment until he had beaten the life out of the poor little creature. In justice to the man—or brute—it should be said that when he found that the child was insensible (it was really dead), he fetched water to bathe its poor battered head; and when he realised that it was dead he cut his own throat and very nearly killed himself— but these considerations seem very little extenuation for the harsh brutality of his conduct. One would have thought that the man who had thus heartlessly tortured to death a helpless child would have been execrated by all men; yet the crowd that assembled at Hunter's execution wore quite a holiday air. There were some 1500 people, most of whom laughed and jested. When the flag was run up there was no demonstration, perhaps the Carlisle people are not demonstrative. However that may be, the contrasted conduct of the crowds at the two executions struck me forcibly; and though it is sad that men should rejoice at the death of a fellow-man, if the cheers had been given at Hunter's death which greeted the death of Lipski, I think they would have been more natural and more English than light jests and laughter.

CHAPTER XIII

INCIDENTS AND ANECDOTES

AS is always the case when a man attains any prominence or notoriety, a number of utterly groundless stories have got afloat about my doings and adventures. Others, which were originally founded on fact, have been so modified and altered that I do not recognise them when they come back to me again. Altogether I have been credited with being the hero of so many surprising adventures that I am afraid the few little incidents which have really occurred to me will seem tame by the side of the fictions.

One of the most striking incidents that ever occurred to me was on the journey from Lincoln to Durham, after executing Mary Lefley, in 1884. At Doncaster we changed from the Great Eastern to the Great Northern Railway. I looked out for a carriage with a vacant corner seat, and got into one containing three rough-looking men. When the train had started they began to talk amongst themselves, and to look at me, and eventually began to chaff me. Of course I pretended not to understand their allusions to the execution that morning, and was indignant at their supposing me to be an executioner, but they were confident that they were right, and began offering to bet amongst themselves as to which of them I should get first. I was glad to get to York, where I parted from their company. Two years afterwards I met the same three men under very different circumstances. They were at Carlisle, condemned to be executed for the Netherby Hall burglary, and I carried out the sentence of the law. Their names were Rudge, Martin, and Baker.

I always try to remain unknown while travelling, but there

is a certain class of people who will always crowd round as if an executioner were a peep-show. On the journey above mentioned, after changing at York, I got into a carriage with a benevolent-looking old gentleman. A little crowd collected round the door, and just as we were starting a porter stuck his head into the window, pointed to my fellow-passenger, and with a silly attempt at jocularity said:—"I hope you'll give him the right tightener." The old gentleman seemed much mystified, and of course I was quite unable to imagine what it meant. At Darlington there was another little crowd, which collected for a short time about our carriage. Fortunately none of the people knew me, so that when the old gentleman asked them what was the matter they could only tell him that Berry was travelling by that train and that they wanted to have a look at him. The old gentleman seemed anxious to see such an awful man as the executioner, and asked me if I should know him if I saw him. I pointed out a low-looking character as being possibly the man, and my fellow-traveller said, "Yes! very much like him." I suppose he had seen a so-called portrait of me in one of the newspapers. We got quite friendly, and when we reached Durham, where I was getting out, he asked for my card. The reader can imagine his surprise when I handed it to him.

This little story has been much warped and magnified, and has even been made the subject of a leading article which takes me to task for "glorying in my gruesome calling," and shocking respectable people by giving them my cards.

Another little anecdote which has been greatly distorted is what I call the toothache story. It happened in 1887, when crossing from Ireland, that there was one of the passengers who was terribly ill with mal de mer and toothache combined. He was rather a bother to several travellers who were not sick, and who wished to enjoy the voyage, and he must have given a lot of trouble to the stewards. I think that one of the latter must have told him that I could cure him, for he came and begged me to tell him what was the best thing for his complaint. I admitted that I was in the habit of giving drops that would instantaneously cure both the toothache and the sea-sickness, but assured him that he would not be willing to take my remedy. Still he persisted, so I handed him a card, and as he was a sensitive man it gave his nerves a shock that was quite sufficient to relieve him of the toothache, and me of his presence for the rest of the voyage. As the card which I then used has often been mentioned in the newspapers, I give a fac-simile of it. The wording was in black, with the fern in green, and the border in gold. I now use a perfectly plain card.

A sad little incident in connection with the murder of Warder Webb by John Jackson will always remain in my memory. I had been to Strangeways Gaol once or twice before on duty, and Webb had always been my personal attendant during my residence, so that we were quite friendly. At the execution previous to Jackson's—that of John Alfred Gell, in May, 1888— we had two or three long chats, and Webb was most anxious that I should go to Manchester to spend a half-day or a day with him in the city, when he could get leave of absence. He hoped it would be a long time before they should see me there again professionally, but said that they would always be glad to see me if I were in Manchester on other business, and could call. Then, turning to the subject of executions, he began wondering who would be the next that I should have to go there for, and who would be the victim, and shaking his head sadly, he said, "A body never knows who will be next." The poor fellow little thought that he would be the next victim, and that the very next time I visited Strangeways would be no friendly call, but a visit to avenge his own death.

Of course, my duties take me about the country a great deal, and I have met a great many interesting people in the course of my travels. As a rule, I do not make myself known unless I have some good reason for doing so, because I have no fancy for making myself into a cheap show. On one occasion I travelled from Coventry to Warwick with the reporter of one of the Coventry papers. He knew nothing of my identity, and does not seem to have recognised me at the execution; but while writing out his report the connection between the gentleman in the train and the executioner in the gaol seems to have dawned upon him, and he wrote the following, which amused me greatly when it appeared in his paper:—

After writing this report and describing the hangman's features and dress, it dawned upon the writer for the first time that the description was that of a gentleman with whom he had travelled from Coventry to Warwick on the previous afternoon. On reflecting upon all the circumstances of the journey, he felt quite certain of the fact; and although amused at the thought of having travelled and conversed with an executioner without knowing it, he was a little chagrined that he had not given the conversation a "professional" turn, which he would have done had he been aware who his fellow traveller was. The incident is sufficient to show that persons travelling by rail occasionally get into singular company without having the slightest knowledge of the fact.

In 1887 when I had to go to Dorchester, to hang Henry William Young for the Poole murder, I stayed at Bournemouth, and took a room in a Temperance Hotel. During the evening I got into conversation with the landlady, who was much interested in the subject of executions, and who appeared to like to discuss it. She was decidedly "down on" Berry, "the hangsman," and expressed herself very freely as to his character and disposition; amongst other pleasant things, saying that he was a man without a soul, and not fit to have intercourse with respectable people. Of course, I smilingly agreed with everything that she had to say, and chuckled quietly to myself about a little surprise that I had in store for her. The surprise came off at bed-time, when she handed me my bedroom candle, and in return I handed her my card. The good lady nearly fainted.

It is not often that I feel frightened, for I am pretty well able to take care of myself, but I once had a little adventure in the train, coming from Galway to Dublin, that gave me one or two cold shivers. It was at a time when Ireland was much disturbed by agrarian outrages, and I knew that amongst some of the lower classes there was a feeling of hatred against myself on account of my occupation. Of this I had an example when going down *to* Galway, and as it led up to, and somewhat prepared me for the other incident, I may as well mention it. My journey to Galway was undertaken for the purpose of hanging four men who were condemned to death for moonlighting. It was an exciting journey altogether, for four men who were in the same compartment as myself from Dublin to Mullingar got into an excited discussion upon some political subject, and just as we left Killucan they began to fight most violently, using their sticks and fists to such an extent that all their faces were soon covered with blood. As the train drew into Mullingar the fury cooled as quickly as it had begun, they all began to apologise to each other and wipe the blood from one another's faces. At Mullingar I got out for a drink, to steady my nerves, for the fight at such close quarters had somewhat upset me, although I took no part in it. On the platform two villainously rough-looking characters spoke a few words to the men who had got out of my compartment and then followed me into the refreshment room, where they seemed anxious to make my acquaintance, and so forcibly insisted that I should have a drink with them, that I had to consent for fear of causing a row. They asked me where I was going, said that they were going to Galway, and in what seemed to me a peculiarly significant tone, asked me if I knew whether Mr. Barry, the hangsman, was really in the train or not. They followed me on to the platform like two shadows, and got into the same compartment of the train. All this made me feel rather uncomfortable, for though I was well armed, there is nothing in life that I dread so much as the possibility of having to kill a man in self-defence and of being tried, and possibly convicted, for murder. I was, therefore, very pleased when two plain-clothes men whom I knew belonged to the Royal Irish Constabulary, got into the other half of the carriage, which was one of those in which there are two compartments divided by a low partition. I do not know whether my two rough companions even noticed that there was anyone in the other half of the carriage, to which their backs were turned. Their conduct, indeed, seemed to show that they thought we were alone, but I could see that the R. I. C. men were regarding them with interest and taking note of every word they said. All the way from Mullingar to Athenry the two fellows plied me with questions, and tried by all means in their power to draw me into discussion, and the expression of opinion. I answered them as briefly as I could without being uncivil, but took care that they should not gain much solid information from my answers. At Athenry they shuffled into the far corner of the compartment, and in stage whispers, which they evidently thought I could not hear, argued as to whether I was "Barry" or not. One of them got quite excited, pointed out that I was an Englishman, that I came from the North of England, that there was no one else in the train that looked like an executioner, that my tale about being a poultry-buyer was "all a loie," and finally that I had a scar on my cheek which "proved it intoirely, begorra!" The other fellow said that "shure the gintleman in the corner was a gintleman, and not a murtherin, blood-thirsty, blagyard of a hangman," which

143

opinion at last seemed to be shared by both. As we steamed into Galway I used my handkerchief, and then rested my hand on the window-ledge with the handkerchief hanging out. This was the signal arranged with my police escort, who were on the platform, and who managed to be just opposite the door when the train stopped. As I marched off amongst those strapping fellows, I looked round to see my two travelling companions gesticulating wildly, and abusing each other for having been deceived, and for having treated "the very blagyard we went to meet." I never knew whether they had intended me any harm, but the constabulary men told me that they were two of the roughest characters in Galway.

The four men who were condemned to death were reprieved, one after the other, as the days fixed for their executions drew near, so that I was not required to carry out my painful duty after all. But I was kept waiting more than a week in Galway gaol, with nothing more lively to do than to read the newspapers, and to walk about in the dreary prison yard, because the governor did not consider that it would be safe for me to venture outside. I was heartily glad when the last reprieve arrived and I was free to return home. To avoid observation as much as possible, I took the midnight train, and as there were very few passengers I secured a compartment to myself, and made all snug for a sleep. I was not disturbed until we reached Mullingar, when I noticed a man who looked into my compartment, then walked the whole length of the train, and finally came into my compartment, although there were others in the train quite empty. He at once began to talk to me in a friendly sort of style, with a strong American twang, but I did not like his looks at all, so pretended to want to go to sleep. As I sized him up from my half-shut lids I set him down as a "heavy swell" Yankee. He wore a big slouch hat and cape coat, carried an elaborately silver-mounted handbag, and his coat pocket showed the unmistakable outline of a revolver. He plied me with all sorts of questions on Irish politics, asked me where I lived, what was my business, where

I was going to stay in Dublin, and a host of other questions which I evaded as far as I decently could. I did tell him, amongst other things, that my name was Aykroyd, and that I lived in the North of England, but not very much beyond this. After a while he pulled out his revolver and commenced examining it in a careless sort of fashion. As I did not like this turn of affairs, I pulled out my own weapon, which was built for business and twice the size of the one carried by the stranger, and made a pretence of looking it over very carefully. The stranger asked me to let him examine my "gun," but I told him that it was a weapon that I did not like to hand about for fear of accidents, and after a final look at the charges, I put it back into my coat pocket in such a position that it covered the stranger, and kept my finger on the trigger until we reached Dublin. The American tried to keep up a conversation all the way, but I was not very encouraging, and I thought that by the time we reached Dublin he would be heartily sick of my company. But when I got out of the station and was driving off to my hotel, I was surprised to find that he jumped on to the same car, and said he would go to the same hotel as I did. After having a wash I came down into the breakfast room and heard the American asking the waitress if she knew Mr. Berry, to which she replied that she did; and then if Mr. Berry was there that morning, to which she replied that she had not seen him. As a matter of fact she had not, and I slipped along the passage to tell her, as she went to the kitchen, that my name, *pro tem*, was Aykroyd. I found in the coffee room that there was a letter addressed to me, on the mantel-piece. The stranger was examining this, and asked me if I knew the hangman by sight. When it was nearly time to catch my boat the stranger still stuck to me, and at the last moment he suggested that we should have a drink together. We went to Mooney's, where I was known to the bar-tender, to whom I tipped a vigorous wink as we went in, which showed him there was something in the wind. After ordering our drinks the American asked him if he knew Berry, the hangman, to which he truthfully replied that he did. The

American then asked if he knew whether Berry had come from Galway by the night mail, adding "he was expected to travel by that train, but Mr. Aykroyd and myself came by it and we saw nobody like him, though I carefully looked along the whole train." The bar-tender of course knew nothing, so we drank up, and I went out to my car, the American shaking hands with me and wishing me a pleasant voyage. I had run it rather close, and quick driving only just brought us to the quay in time for me to get aboard. As the ship swung out from the quay-side, a car, driven at red-hot speed, came dashing along, and the passenger, whom I recognised as my American, gesticulated wildly, as if he wanted the vessel to stop. But we swung out with steam and tide, and he drove some distance along the quay-sides wildly but vainly waving his hands.

The next time I was at Mooney's I heard some further particulars. The stranger had gone back for another drink, and after chatting for a few minutes, the bar-tender told him that his friend Mr. Aykroyd was the very Berry for whom he had been enquiring. On hearing that, he rapped out half-a-dozen oaths, rushed for a car, and drove off in mad haste.

I have never seen him since, nor has the bar-tender, and I never knew what were the motives for his peculiar conduct.

APPENDIX

THE TROUBLE WITH "ANSWERS" LIMITED

EARLY last year (1890) I felt compelled to bring an action for libel against the "Answers" Newspaper Co., Ltd. As the case was fully reported at the time, I think that a report condensed from the columns of *The Bradford Observer*, of March 17th, 1890, may be more satisfactory than my own statement of the case. I, therefore, give it, in the form of an appendix, rather than in the chapter—"The Press and the Public"—to which it belongs.

In this action Mr. Waddy, Q.C., M.P., and Mr. Waugh (instructed by Mr. J. J. Wright) appeared for the plaintiff, Mr. James Berry, the public executioner, of 1, Bilton Place, Bradford; and Mr. Cyril Dodd, Q.C., appeared for the defendants, the "Answers" Newspaper Company, Limited. The plaintiff claimed £500 for libel, which was printed and published in the periodical called "Answers;" the defendants admitted the printing and publication of the libel, and by way of mitigation of damages they withdrew all moral imputations against Berry's character and paid a sum of 40s. into court, and apologised for the words used.

Mr. Waddy said in behalf of the plaintiff—and he thought the observation would commend itself to their judgment—that no man in the kingdom, whatever he might be, and whatever calling he might follow, as long as he followed the duties of his calling in honesty and integrity, ought to be deliberately insulted and flouted for any reason whatever; and he believed that when they heard what kinds of falsehoods were printed concerning Berry they would agree with him that Mr. Berry, although he was the common executioner, being a sober and respectable man, was entitled at their hands to be protected from wanton insult. He would tell them what the facts were. It appeared that some time in September or October of 1889 a man named White came to him representing himself to be a correspondent of an American newspaper, and told Mr. Berry that he was anxious to hear his views upon the very interesting subject of executions by means of electricity, and that his opinion, in view of his experience at executions, was of very great importance. He offered Mr. Berry a fee of £3 if he would give him the interview which he desired; and that fee was paid, and Mr. Berry did discuss the question with him. He did that on the promise, both by word of mouth and in writing, that whatever he said should not be published in this country. Mr. Waddy then read the article which had appeared in "Answers," from which I need only give extracts.

He is a powerful, thick-set man, of about medium stature, and his countenance is not an unpleasant one at a first glance, though upon closer study one discovers that the face reveals the lack of several moral elements in the man's composition, which seems to indicate that the Creator designed him especially for the ends he serves.

A critical observer would probably say that his eyes are too close together, and that their brilliancy is that of the codfish rather than the eagle, while, though the mouth and chin indicate determination, the forehead gives the impression of lack of balance.

A phrenologist would perhaps find that the cranial bumps that indicate sense and shame, pity and sympathy, are not particularly well developed upon the head of Mr. Berry.

"Have you ever been threatened by the friends of criminals whom you have hanged?"

"Often," replied Mr. Berry, "but I don't pay no attention to them. I'm a doin' o' my duty, and I'm protected by th' Government."

"It was said that if Mrs. Maybrick had not been reprieved a mob would have been formed in Liverpool to prevent your hanging her."

"They'd never have seen me," said Mr. Berry, "I'd 'a been in th' jail and 'anged her before th' mob knew I was about, and I'd been on th' train and on my way back 'ome before they knew she was dead. Why when I 'anged Poole in Dublin, who murdered informer Kenny—O'Donnell, who murdered th' other informer, Carey, having been 'anged at Newgate th' day before—there was a great mob in Dublin to prevent my getting into th' prison, and nobody outside knew Poole was 'anged until I was on th' boat a steaming away for Holyhead."

"How do you manage that?" I asked again.

"I'll tell you," said Mr. Berry in a burst of confidence. "I shaves off my whiskers and I puts on women's clothes. That's th' way I got into Dublin Jail, with my ropes and straps under my clothes, and that's th' way I've done many a job."

Berry never did such a thing in his life as put on women's clothes. He never had occasion to put them on, and there was not the slightest shadow of foundation for the statement. The people mentioned in the article as having been hanged by Berry were not hanged by him at all. This libel was printed upon November 23rd, 1889, and an action was commenced at once. The defendants now stated in mitigation of damages that they denied that the words bore the construction which the plaintiff had put upon them, withdrew all imputations, and admitted that any such were unfounded, and apologised for the matter complained of. But the apology and the withdrawal appeared upon the pleadings only. From that day to this, with 158,000 of their papers going out every week, there had net been one single word in the paper apologising for their action. It was open to them with a view to mitigation of damages, to have taken this course, but they had done nothing but put their apology upon the record, and paid into court the majestic sum of 40s. as, in their opinion, sufficient to atone for the wrong.

Mr. Berry was then put into the box and supported Mr. Waddy's statements.

Mr. Waddy then spoke upon the whole case.

For the defendants Mr. Dodd said that the owners of the newspaper which he represented were as anxious as anybody could be that reasonable justice should be done. Of course, Berry did not suggest that there was any actual money out-of-pocket loss. Then another feature of such a case was the question of whether the paper was one of that class which feeds on personal attacks. He submitted that the general character of the paper, a point to which juries were apt to pay some attention, was good. The articles in question were copied from an American paper, and the proprietors of "Answers" were in the position of having been misled, just as the proprietors of the *New York Sun* had been misled by the large imagination of Mr. White. Berry seemed to be very quick in his methods, for his writ was served within a very few days of the appearance of the article, and without any opportunity being given to his clients to try and make some kind of apology to suit him. His clients had endeavoured to meet the case in a perfectly reasonable way. They did not for a moment express any doubt that they were dealing with an honest, a decent, and an experienced man, they withdrew all supposed imputations, and had had no intention of making any; and he contended that the highest testimonial possible was one from a person who had said something derogatory to him. Berry had suffered no monetary damage whatever beyond the actual costs of the action. He suggested, therefore, that the jury should give such a verdict as would show that the plaintiff was quite right in bringing the matter into court, but that they were of opinion that the defendants had done everything that they could to mitigate the mischief and annoyance occasioned by the publication of the libel.

His Lordship then summed up, and the jury found for the plaintiff, with £100 damages.